The Declaration of Transformation:
Grounds for Immediate Constitutional Change

By
James S. Sitnik

For permission requests, email the publisher *at* Transformation@DeclarationOf.com .
Check online for permission forms, information, etc at
www.DeclarationOf.com

Published by JSMP, LLC
First edition

All rights reserved.

Proofreading consultant: FirstEditing

ISBN-13: 978-1519191878
ISBN-10: 1519191871

www.DeclarationOf.com

Illustrations by: Ian Aprecio

In memory of my beloved mother, Annette Sitnik...

and my Aunt Freda and Uncle Dick.

TABLE OF CONTENTS

INTRODUCTION

This book is meant to be analyzed and discussed. Take your notes. Study ideas. Write and record your current thoughts. Read philosophies and texts on governments. Find affirming and opposing ideas and examples. Critically examine these ideas. Deep think about causes and effects. Write and note significate dialogs for yourself. Create solutions and record them in your notebook.

The main point of the book is to encourage the arrangement of a Constitutional Convention of the states. Focusing on one point or issue within the book without keeping the big-picture goal in mind will do you a disservice to your analysis.

I hope you will gain insight and awareness, and become involved in stimulating conversations after reading this book. And lastly, after reading this book, my further hope is that you will become an activist for Constitutional change.

SPECIAL NOTES FOR THIS EDITION:

Write and mark in this book. Use persistent attention to evalualate. Initiate movement of the mind. Grip differ views. Oscillate assessments in term of:

- Founding Fathers' views
- World history/Past democracies comparisons
- Social psycology
- Individual's steadfast mind set verses changing mind sets
- Finacial vs economic views
- Business management and organization
- English Literature
- A "New Age Founding Fathers" view

Special Thanks:

Thanks to a friend who extensively helped me navigate through most English grammar landmines.

Thanks to the Reform Party of the early 1990s for your efforts in trying to head off the financial situation our country now finds itself in today.

The Hard Evidence

EXHIBIT A – (for your examination)

States' Share of **18 Trillion** Dollar National Debt

State	Estimated Population 2014*	Percent of Total US Population	State's Share of 18 Trillion Dollar Debt (Approximation)
California	38,802,500	12.17%	$2,190,464,000,000
Texas	26,956,958	8.45%	$1,521,764,000,000
Florida	19,893,297	6.24%	$1,123,009,000,000
New York	19,746,227	6.19%	$1,114,707,000,000
Illinois	12,880,580	4.04%	$727,130,000,000
Pennsylvania	12,787,209	4.01%	$721,859,000,000
Ohio	11,594,163	3.64%	$654,509,000,000
Georgia	10,097,343	3.17%	$570,011,000,000
North Carolina	9,943,964	3.12%	$561,353,000,000
Michigan	9,909,877	3.11%	$559,429,000,000
New Jersey	8,938,175	2.80%	$504,575,000,000
Virginia	8,326,289	2.61%	$470,033,000,000
Washington	7,061,530	2.21%	$398,635,000,000
Massachusetts	6,745,408	2.12%	$380,789,000,000
Arizona	6,731,484	2.11%	$380,003,000,000
Indiana	6,596,855	2.07%	$372,403,000,000
Tennessee	6,549,352	2.05%	$369,722,000,000
Missouri	6,063,589	1.90%	$342,299,000,000
Maryland	5,976,407	1.87%	$337,378,000,000
Wisconsin	5,757,564	1.81%	$325,024,000,000
Minnesota	5,457,173	1.71%	$308,066,000,000
Colorado	5,355,866	1.68%	$302,347,000,000
Alabama	4,849,377	1.52%	$273,755,000,000
South Carolina	4,832,482	1.52%	$272,801,000,000
Louisiana	4,649,676	1.46%	$262,482,000,000
Kentucky	4,413,457	1.38%	$249,147,000,000
Oregon	3,970,239	1.25%	$224,126,000,000

State	Estimated Population 2014 *	Percent of Total Population	State's Share of 18 Trillion Dollar Debt
Oklahoma	3,878,051	1.22%	$218,922,000,000
Connecticut	3,596,677	1.13%	$203,038,000,000
Puerto Rico	3,548,397	1.11%	$200,313,000,000
Iowa	3,107,126	0.97%	$175,402,000,000
Mississippi	2,994,079	0.94%	$169,021,000,000
Arkansas	2,966,369	0.93%	$167,456,000,000
Utah	2,942,902	0.92%	$166,132,000,000
Kansas	2,904,021	0.91%	$163,937,000,000
Nevada	2,839,099	0.89%	$160,272,000,000
New Mexico	2,085,572	0.65%	$117,734,000,000
Nebraska	1,881,503	0.59%	$106,214,000,000
West Virginia	1,850,326	0.58%	$104,454,000,000
Idaho	1,634,464	0.51%	$92,268,000,000
Hawaii	1,419,561	0.45%	$80,137,000,000
Maine	1,330,089	0.42%	$75,086,000,000
New Hampshire	1,326,813	0.42%	$74,901,000,000
Rhode Island	1,055,173	0.33%	$59,566,000,000
Montana	1,023,579	0.32%	$57,783,000,000
Delaware	935,614	0.29%	$52,817,000,000
South Dakota	853,175	0.27%	$48,163,000,000
North Dakota	739,482	0.23%	$41,745,000,000
Alaska	736,732	0.23%	$41,590,000,000
D.C.	658,893	0.21%	$37,196,000,000
Vermont	626,562	0.20%	$35,370,000,000
Wyoming	584,153	0.18%	$32,976,000,000

*Estimate of 2014 population of each state, and estimate of total US population for 2014 (which was used to calculate the percentage of population for each state was from from www.census.gov.

EXHIBIT B – (for your examination)
Accumulated Trade Deficits Since 1976

Year	Annual Trade Balance [1]	Cumulative Balance
1976	-$6,082,000	-$6,082,000
1977	-$27,246,000	-$33,328,000
1978	-$29,763,000	-$63,091,000
1979	-$24,565,000	-$87,656,000
1980	-$19,407,000	-$107,063,000
1981	-$16,172,000	-$123,235,000
1982	-$24,156,000	-$147,391,000
1983	-$57,767,000	-$205,158,000
1984	-$109,072,000	-$314,230,000
1985	-$121,880,000	-$436,110,000
1986	-$138,538,000	-$574,648,000
1987	-$151,684,000	-$726,332,000
1988	-$114,566,000	-$840,898,000
1989	-$93,141,000	-$934,039,000
1990	-$80,864,000	-$1,014,903,000
1991	-$31,135,000	-$1,046,038,000
1992	-$39,212,000	-$1,085,250,000
1993	-$70,311,000	-$1,155,561,000
1994	-$98,493,000	-$1,254,054,000
1995	-$96,384,000	-$1,350,438,000
1996	-$104,065,000	-$1,454,503,000
1997	-$108,273,000	-$1,562,776,000
1998	-$166,140,000	-$1,728,916,000
1999	-$263,160,000	-$1,992,076,000
2000	-$376,749,000	-$2,368,825,000
2001	-$361,771,000	-$2,730,596,000
2002	-$417,432,000	-$3,148,028,000

---

[1] Yearly balance from: https://www.census.gov/foreign-trade/statistics/historical/gands.pdf

Year	Annual Trade Balance [2]	Cumulative Balance
2003	-$490,984,000	-$3,639,012,000
2004	-$605,357,000	-$4,244,369,000
2005	-$708,624,000	-$4,952,993,000
2006	-$753,288,000	-$5,706,281,000
2007	-$696,728,000	-$6,403,009,000
2008	-$698,338,000	-$7,101,347,000
2009	-$379,154,000	-$7,480,501,000
2010	-$494,737,000	-$7,975,238,000
2011	-$559,880,000	-$8,535,118,000
2012	-$540,362,000	-$9,075,480,000
2013	-$476,392,000	**-$9,551,872,000**

[2] Yearly balance from: https://www.census.gov/foreign-trade/statistics/historical/gands.pdf

Part 1.
Grievances against the Democratic and Republican Parties

There comes a time in the lifecycle of human democracy and human events, when government becomes over-responsible for its people, and the people become under-responsible for themselves, *and* when elder citizens take from the country's future generations without regard. These are the characteristics of the last phase of a living democracy. In human history, no democracy or federated republic has had in place a system to avoid this last phase.

These "over and under" responsibilities have become a matter of seemingly unbreakable habit and unwavering expectations by the citizens that rule, the citizens that are governed, and the citizens that directly influence all branches and sub-branches of government. The two national ruling parties of this nation thrive on these habits and the citizen's inability to change and to recognize what change is needed. The deep-thinking minds that created the Declaration of Independence so say that mankind is more willing to put up with injustices and evils—and bad government—than to change away from these familiar thinking patterns and habits "and make themselves upright." We should strive to not make this statement true.

The two great national political parties of this day, Democratic and Republican, that rule this Union of 50 states, in their hubris, use obfuscation and thick bureaucracy of their own making to hide their faults from the citizens and from themselves. They have solidified an environment in which past attempts for corrective course change have failed. They are unable to recognize or do anything about their habits, which continue the status quo of fiduciary evils and pernicious politics. This results in the blinding of the great two national parties and their constituencies as to the consequences and penalties of consistent and persistent trade

deficits, and blistering financial deficits.

Let there be no mistake; the two national parties have been building potential energies for decades that will surreptitiously undermine the domestic tranquility, common defense, general welfare, absolute liberties, and pursuits of happiness that they are supposed to protect! Thus, these two parties are in gross violation of the Constitution.

As the Declaration of Independence lists grievances against the governance of King George, this document, The Declaration of Transformation, lists grievances against the governance of the Democratic and Republican parties. It proves without prejudice the lack of prudence and foresight these two parties possess in the ruling of the country. The list exposes their policies and processes, which build up the latent means for shattering the human rights of all the citizens of this country and dissolving the current and future adhesiveness of the Union—currently holding at 50 states.

Here, for your deep and serious consideration, are the grievances:

THE GRIEVANCES

1. They have refused to balance the budget.

2. They have violated their own laws concerning budgets.

3. They raid and encourage the pillaging of the Treasury; they are using up all the creditworthiness of the country. Moreover, in their habits, they will continue these actions without pausing.

4. They, by creating the astronomical national debt, are destroying the future human rights of their constituents. One of the wickedest behaviors of ANY form of

government—be it democracy, socialism, communism, monarchy, oligarchy, or dictatorship—is shackling their citizens in extreme debt. The lack of foresight and financial wisdom by the two political parties is nothing less than outrageous, and shows total contempt for ordinary citizens and their families.

5. They let themselves be influenced by lobbyists by accepting "legal" gifts. Then they support lobbyists by passing bills with hidden line items that give the lobbyists money, benefits, or additional influence, which hurts the finances of the country.

6. They are incapable of accepting the fact that government itself is an expense on the people. Thus, they are unable to find firm reason to cut government spending and balance the budget.

7. They have repeatedly misrepresented the financial situation of the country; they continue to assert in State of the Union addresses how rich the country is, despite a huge national debt and the loss of our hard currency to international trade.

8. They have thrown us into grand, lengthy, unwarranted, and expensive wars for which no citizen wants to pay taxes. In addition, there is and will be little or no benefit from even winning such wars, yet they continue to spend huge sums of money on war. They have and are squandering our limited defense resources.

9. They have removed sturdy financial regulations put in place since the last depression.

10. They have spread economic propaganda among the citizens that "a penny SPENT is a penny earned," foolishly contradicting one of the wisest of all the Founding Fathers—Mr. Benjamin Franklin.

11. They have created an environment where the United States is enormously reliant on foreign manufacturing, which weakens the nation's current and future security and economy. They have disregarded the long-standing wisdom of Alexander Hamilton's 11-point plan for enhancing the American economy through manufacturing (which was encouraged by President George Washington.[3])[4]

12. They do nothing to prevent foreigners from buying US companies, thereby giving foreigners a pathway to influencing the functions of our government—its laws, regulations, trade agreements, and budgets.

13. They do not see the appalling irony of borrowing money from foreign countries in the name of the citizens, only to give that money to other foreign countries. Then at the same time, they ignore the financial difficulties of their own states from which money must come to pay back the

---

[3] "He [Washington] thought that Congress should be empowered to foster domestic manufacturing industries as a means of lessening the importation of foreign goods." Nettels, Curtis P., *George Washington: First President of the United States*, The Erastus Granger Papers-A Digital Library, Burton, Anthony, Kiernan Colin, Van Gilder, Gerald B., Jr.
www.oswego.edu/library2/archives/digital_collections/granger/georgewashingto.html

[4] Hartmann, Thom, Berrett-Koehler Publishers, Book Excerpt, *Eleven Ways to Rebuild Our Country*,
http://truth-out.org/archive/component/k2/item/92730-eleven-ways-to-rebuild-our-country, Nov 08, 2010.

1   borrowed money.

2   14. They, with great duplicity and misguided intent, overrate
3   the safety and well-being of U.S. Savings bonds and
4   Treasury bonds.

5   15. They condone the action of former representatives and
6   their staffs to be hired by lobbyists to find ways to take
7   advantage of the people's governmental system. The two
8   parties fail to recognize, acknowledge, and take action
9   against this kind of political corruption committed by
10   their own former political partners. This endorses a lack
11   of ethics and virtues throughout the two-party political
12   system, which adds to the processes that are destined to
13   destroy this country. Former representatives helping
14   lobbyists or becoming lobbyists should instead be
15   interpreted as a treasonable act.

16   16. The two national parties have no plan, no proposal, and
17   no blueprint for repaying money borrowed from foreign
18   countries. If we as a country do not give these foreign
19   countries the financial justice they deserve, the growth of
20   their animosity, belligerence, and possibly physical
21   hostilities will be directed squarely on US families. The
22   two parties have not been protecting the future of
23   American families—they have been betraying them.

24   17. They have failed thoroughly and utterly to make our
25   country energy independent, in spite of taking the country
26   trillions of dollars into debt. The amount of reliance we
27   have on foreign oil is obscene. The two parties have
28   invested in the country badly and have shown they lack
29   the leadership to make this country energy independent,

thereby weakening our position of being a free country.

18. They write long, unreadable bills that are then used to hide improper and inappropriate rules, regulations, tax loopholes, and budget irregularities. This increases the apathy in the common citizen towards government— exactly what many lobbyists hope for.

19. They have made the tax code exceedingly complex, far beyond what many people can manage. It is imbalanced, unreadable, and adds burden to the most conscientious of tax-paying citizens and businesses that do pay and want to pay their fair share of tax.

20. They have not stopped at the tax code; they have made health care reform exceedingly complex, far beyond what any country can manage. It is imbalanced, unreadable, and adds burdens to the most conscientious of employers, insurance carriers, health care providers, as well as citizens.

21. They have allowed horrendous trade agreements to exist for decades, yielding unrelenting trade deficits that impoverish the nation; the two parties have ignored this pouring out of cash from the American economy. In addition, the decrease in the standard of living that should have been the accompanying result of these trade agreements is being artificially offset by the government borrowing and printing huge sums of money that is thrown out into the economy. The long-term damage to the economy due to these trade agreements and artificial economic counterweights are immense. (See Exhibit B.)

22. They have instituted poor checks and balances on the financial management of the individual spheres of government—entitlements, federal departments, the military, and foreign aid. Television news programs have been documenting this waste of money for decades. The operations of the government financial system have been so perverted for so long that it has become routine and is not questioned; it seems to be non-correctable. The two parties seem very comfortable with this nefarious situation.

23. They refuse to recognize the momentous shift in the economic and financial position of the country that began in 1976[5] as the nation went from a trade surplus nation to a trade deficit nation.[6] For almost 40 years they have continued to make economic and financial decisions as if the nation had trade surpluses rather than trade deficits. Therefore, not only did they not act quickly and decisively to reverse this critical economic statistic in 1976, they have been completely ignoring it for decades since! The two national parties plainly do not have the business acumen to run the nation. However they do know how to fill their own pockets,.

24. They refused to decrease defense spending and scale

---

5 See: https://www.census.gov/foreign-trade/statistics/historical/gands.pdf
6 In business this is called a "strategic inflection point" - a dramatic change in the environment that makes us alter the way we do things or else risk extinction. *Strategic Thinking Skills* by Professor Stanley K. Ridgley (Audio CD through The Great Courses). There are numerous companies that faced one or more "strategic inflection points" during their existence. They have been in the headlines in recent years. Examples include a movie camera and film company, several computer companies, and a coffee company.

down the military after the end of the Cold War with the Soviet Union. This irresponsible management decision has recklessly and significantly added to the debt, which set the stage for the current culture of military overspending. This overspending has drained our limited defense resources that will be needed in the future.

25. They intentionally disregard the fact that rich countries do not go trillions of dollars in debt. They refuse to see that to be rich, a country must have surpluses. They refuse to acknowledge that debt is a nemesis of freedom.

26. They wrongly believe they can control the economy; they mistakenly believe they cannot control the finances.

27. They make American businesses less competitive both at home and abroad by increasing the minimum wage, which has forced many businesses over the decades to either move jobs from America to other countries—or else become extinct. This situation significantly reduces the opportunities for trade surpluses, which is critical for growing the economy without having the government borrow money. The loss of jobs is concealed by the government borrowing money, which is used to create government jobs—jobs that do not create a trade surplus for the country.

28. They have made it difficult for the common US citizen to compete for the finite number of jobs available worldwide by increasing the minimum wage in this country while disregarding the fact that the minimum wage in many other countries is much lower and remains mostly stagnant.

29. For more than thirty years the two parties, with great negligence and obliviousness, have created economic and financial policies that advance Osama Bin Laden's dream—bankrupting the United States.[7]

30. They refuse to add significant control to the southern border, while punishing those states that try to protect the border or try to discourage unlawful immigration. Without controls on the border, the increased population will strain the social services paid for by the taxpayers, who are already on the hook for trillions of dollars of debt. Eventually this will cause the extinction of food stamps, welfare, and heath care services our own citizens need. Yet, the two parties will continue their mismanaging of the nation's borders for the sake of special interest groups rather than protecting the future of the country.

31. They give conflicting financial management advice to citizens. "Save for retirement" they advise. But then the two political parties turn around and increase the minimum wage, making the money that was saved by citizens worth less! In the same breath, the parties say "spend money" so our economy will be strong. But then they make trade agreements with other countries whose products are cheaper than American-made products, causing citizens to spend money on these foreign products. The money then leaves the country, weakening our economy! These are two examples of the two political parties' incompetent and uncoordinated financial

---

[7] "Al-Qaida will bankrupt America, bin Laden says," by Donna Bryson, Associated Press, *Rocky Mountain News*, Tuesday, November 2, 2004.

management philosophies. The two parties are financially
dysfunctional.

32. They have artificially created the last 30-some-year rise in
the stock market by borrowing money and just
"throwing" it out into the economy. They have had no
thought and no plan for creating self-sustaining, long-
term economic growth with the money. This is financial
mismanagement at its worst.

33. They have replaced a drafted army with a professional
volunteer army, and have used it as a way to disconnect
or reduce the common citizen's emotional and intellectual
involvement in the nation's military decisions. This
impairs the citizen's natural tendency to scrutinize and
critique military actions, which would then be used to
influence our political representatives. This scheme allows
the two parties to use military action with near impunity,
as there are fewer annoyances from "irritating" anti-war
groups. The two parties have eliminated the critical check
and balance that a drafted army brings, which is essential
for the continued existence of a self-ruling republic.

34. The two parties have allowed the waste of huge sums of
borrowed money on special projects—many of them are
military. Many of these projects have had huge cost
overruns, and have created faulty equipment or
infrastructure that cannot be used or is not needed.
Numerous examples of this pattern of bad financial
management by the two governing parties have been
documented throughout the last several decades by the
news media. Furthermore, the scheme of spending
borrowed money instead of increasing taxes to pay for

these expenditures hides the real cost of these projects from the citizens, and disconnects the common citizen from the effects of the parties' gross financial mismanagement. The result is that the two parties are allowed to act with impunity and have opened the door to widespread corruption in Washington, DC.

35. For decades, despite citizens demanding low taxes, the two parties increased spending and the indebtedness of the nation to the point where citizens will be obligated to pay much, much, more in taxes either through conventional taxes, or through the use of immense hyper-inflationary manipulations, or both.

36. The two parties have failed to notice and make changes to the law that prevents states that have their own large financial debt from having undeserved influence on the budget of the United States. It is an outrageous conflict of interest for these states to vote on the country's financial matters.

37. The two parties have misled the people into thinking they are guaranteed to receive "entitlements" such as Social Security, health care, pensions, food stamps, jobs, etc., when in fact there is no guarantee. In addition, the two parties have been mismanaging the finances of the nation so badly that all these important benefits run the risk of being wiped out. This is another demonstration of the horrible leadership these two parties are providing its citizens.

38. They have turned laissez-faire upside down by bailing out Wall Street firms, while not providing a trustworthy and

reliable way to regulate these firms' veracity in financial dealings.

39. The two national parties and their lobbyists manipulate state governors and legislatures into ignoring the dire financial situation of the nation. The states essentially bow down like servants to the central government so they can receive tainted money for the people of their state. The two parties encourage the disconnection of the state governors and legislatures, keeping them from acting as a check and balance on the power of the central government—a duty that was unwritten in the Constitution, but implied in the Founding Father's documents. The two national parties and their lobbyists will fight to maintain this disconnect, to the detriment of the future of the nation.

40. They have promised government workers generous pensions that the taxpayers do not have the ability to support.

41. For decades they have been willing to compromise with each other and saddle the people with slave-inducing debt instead of finding ways to amass liberty-stimulating surpluses.

42. They refuse to acknowledge the natural cycles of economic expansion and contraction when making budgetary and financial decisions for the nation. Because of this, they have been severely undermining the economy instead of protecting it.

43. They fail to comprehend that they are not the stock

market; they are not a charity; they are not the sole
provider; they are not "the economy."

44. They force employers who need to hire people for low-paying jobs to look for and hire illegal immigrants, when instead the employers should be hiring US citizens. The two parties support this system by paying citizens not to work by issuing food stamps, shelling out lengthy unemployment payments, and providing other government giveaways. These payments encourage many citizens to take a free ride and avoid financial responsibility. Because taxpaying citizens are not paying enough in taxes to cover these payments, these expenses increase the national debt—putting more pressure on future working taxpayers and hurting the country as a whole. The two parties do not seem to realize these debt-producing payments cannot go on forever without causing severe economic repercussions.

45. They have neglected to create functional mechanisms and processes that control and monitor the federal agencies that would ensure the agencies do not violate citizens' rights, international law, and Constitutional law, as well as misuse money. Recent IRS and NSA abuses are examples of continuing exploitation for which the two parties refuse to create solutions.

46. They have ignorantly equated money received from selling US products and services abroad with money invested in this country by foreign countries. The financial differences between these types of income are great. Foreign investments are designed to drain more currency out of this country, eventually draining this

economy. The selling of products and services to other countries brings money into this economy and strengthens it. The misunderstanding the two parties have on the two distinct sources of money demonstrates their inability to be fiduciary managers for the country.

47. They have created voting pools—groups of people who vote based on their entitlements, grants, contracts, loans, paychecks, and other government benefits. This creates a huge conflict of interest, as there are no checks and balances from keeping these voting pools from voting to increase their own benefits at the expense of other citizens; there are no checks and balances to protect the national treasury from being emptied by these voting pools; there are no checks and balances to protect the credit worthiness of the nation from these voting pools. The two parties have ignored the deleterious effect this has on the future of the nation.

48. They have permitted the country to exceed the maximum ideal population (MIP) for the given land size, the quantity of natural resources (such as water and natural gas), and number of jobs available. This is being done by allowing millions of illegal immigrants to come over the border.

49. The two national parties surreptitiously, with the sleight-of-hand of a scam artist, manipulate the citizens into focusing their attention on the numbers in their IRAs, 401(k), and Social Security accounts, rather than focusing on what the two parties are doing to the financial balance sheet of the nation.

50. They have created a global atmosphere of ill will towards our country by failing to apply the golden rule: treat other countries as we want to be treated; treat other governments as we want to be treated.

51. The two parties falsely proselytize that a Constitutional Convention by the states is dangerous and unnecessary, and the Constitution should remain a static document only to be changed by Congress. This is a disingenuous warning coupled with habitual hubris.

52. Members of both parties voted for the worst financial mistake involving the military in US history—the invasion of Iraq. Moreover, the two parties have cloaked this fact by borrowing money instead of raising taxes to pay for the expense of the war. The borrowing of money keeps citizens from fully comprehending this horrendous financial mistake; this in turn enables congressional representatives who voted for this serious mistake to remain in power. Such a disastorous mistake against our country should demand that all representatives who voted for the war be voted out of power by the citizens.

53. They are oblivious to the decades of gradual and systematic means that they themselves have incorporated in their governance to weaken the reasons states should stay in the Union.

54. The two parties give out student loans for degrees for which a job cannot be had. This leads to the inability of former students to pay back the loans, which in turn adds to the national debt. But then the two parties allow legal immigrants to come in to fill skilled jobs for which

students who received student loans have not the skills. This irony falls into the parties' continued pattern of mismanagement, and again demonstrates their inability to rule with wisdom.

55. The two parties lack the foresight of the country's Founding Fathers—a sine qua non leadership quality for maintaining a free republic into the far future. They leave the country's future completely to fate rather than to plan.

❧

GRIEVANCES OF THE YOUNGEST GENERATION AGAINST THE TWO POWERFUL POLITICAL PARTIES:

In the last phases of a living democracy, the older generation takes from the younger. Therefore, this brings forth a new list of grievances. Speaking for the younger generation:

56. At our future expense, the two parties have made themselves and their older constituents comfortable. They have done this by borrowing money over the last 35 years in our name. By not requiring the generations that came before us to pay enough taxes to cover spending, the two parties increase the financial burden on us. The refusal of the leaders of both parties to reduce the borrowing of money is undisputable proof they do not care for the younger generations.

57. They do not support real change that would safeguard

our generation's future economy, our future military
defense, our future human rights, and our future country.

58. They care not for future generations to start on an equal
financial footing as have older generations. They have put
us in a vast financial hole.

59. They have unethically spent our future paychecks even
before we are/were at an age where we can get a job, or
are eligible to vote.

60. They want us to pay extra-high taxes to cover the older
generation's entitlements, while the older generation gives
us the debt in return.

61. They give entitlements to older generations to which they
are not entitled. The money for older generations'
entitlements should instead be used to pay down the
national debt that their generation accepted when they
were younger.

62. The two parties do not realize a generation cannot build
from debt unless that debt is invested where it yields
surpluses. Their negligence and ineptitude has failed to
secure our financial future.

❧

"*P*rudence indeed, will dictate that Governments long established should not be changed for light and transient causes…" This was written by the authors of the Declaration of Independence. However, let the citizens of this country— and any citizen in any country on this earth—be the witness; this document does not hold "light or transient causes," but serious, vital, and moral causes.

For more than three decades and five presidential administrations, appeals and attempts by small numbers of politicians, citizen groups, and other political parties have failed to have the slightest influence on the two national parties' spending attitudes and political habits. The Democratic and Republican national parties are, in effect, deaf, dumb, and blind to suggestions of financial responsibility. The natural economic outcome of the two parties' habit of spending borrowed money while declaring, "The country is rich," will be the cause of great financial oppression upon every citizen of every state. Let there be no doubt—these two national ruling parties are unfit to continue to lead the Union of free people.

The situation demands that certain powers and responsibilities need to be removed from the central government and assigned to the states and citizens. This means altering the Constitution and this can only be happen with citizen involvement.

Can citizens really change their government? The Founding Fathers make mention in the Declaration of Independence that humans have a great propensity not to change their government (or themselves), even if obvious and drastic change is admittedly needed. However, if any citizens in any country in the world can produce conscious, mindful,

civil, bold, and peaceful change, the American citizen can.

Unless responsibility is taken away from this central government by the initiating actions of responsible citizens, cities, counties, and states, and unless noble and intentional sacrifice of finances and of personal fortune is made by American citizens and their businesses as a whole, this democracy, this republic, will dissolve and be abandoned once the outcome of the nation's financial irresponsibility is fully felt. Other forms of much less freedom-loving governments and more importantly, forms of much less peaceful governments will fill its void. The Constitution itself will become void. Our children will lose the means and ways to pursue happiness. The populace will no longer be called Americans.

With this course of human events in motion, what should a people do? The situation calls for the many citizens who have been absent from the political scene and who know this list of grievances to be true, to begin to act outside of their own current political and economic habits and mind-sets. They must begin to take action that will begin the process of proper, structured change for the nation. They must search for and find "New Age Founding Fathers."

Be on notice—the two national parties and their paying lobbyists will curse proper changes to the Constitution. They will continue to try, using a variety of means, to deceive the citizens into becoming complacent and content and try to stop change from happening. They will say, "We agree with the changes, BUT…"—the "BUT" being used more as a superficial excuse for not making changes rather than stating legitimate arguments. These tactics should not deceive citizens. Citizens should not let the power of the two national parties impede and obstruct actions that are

honorable, right, and moral.

With that in mind, citizens should also be aware that there will always be legitimate counterarguments. These have to be evaluated, similar to the way our Founding Fathers weighed the arguments for and against articles in the Constitution.

Citizens should know without a doubt that future generations would honor and revere their actions of standing up to these two powerful parties and changing the Constitution. Citizens should realize this is for their descendants.

Armed with reasons based on the list of grievances, citizens must acquire the moral courage to change the Constitution in order to break the corrupted habits (both financial and political) of the two national parties. There is little choice but to support the broad transformation of the US Constitution. Citizens should be encouraged that the Founding Fathers would support citizens that are for the cause of saving the Union through a great transformation.

With great effort and with firm faith on the new fortifications from the heavens, the New Age Founding Fathers must commit themselves to the cause of American financial restoration in order to preserve and protect the liberty of the citizens for generations to come. In the face of the great challenges to come that will test our hearts and souls, let us make ourselves upright; let us recommit to keeping together the Union of 50 individual states, and let us be called Americans always.

❧

Part 2.
New Age Amendments to the Constitution

ॐ

Change or be changed. We the people of the United States must either institute change or be the victim of change; no other options exist.

The Founding Fathers of this nation left an insidious hole in the Constitution. This was echoed in a warning by the Founding Fathers themselves: "It is unwise and improvident to vest in the general government a power to borrow at discretion, without any limitation or restriction."[8] This statement in the Anti-Federalist Papers is a foretold story of our nation's current state of financial affairs. This power of unlimited borrowing has allowed the actions of the two political parties to put us in a deep financial abyss—an abyss that can thwart freedom. The Constitution is void of any checks and balances or limitations concerning borrowing money. This should be self-evident to all citizens; it has been exposed and in plain sight for decades. This situation demands that change take place. And it will, either through citizens' initiatives or by the force of ordinary financial principles.

Change will occur:

- because citizens in government (in both political and bureaucratic positions) irresponsibly spend astronomical amounts of borrowed money for which there is little return on investment;

- because the number of citizens demanding government benefits and handouts—deserved or not, needed or

---

[8] The Founding Fathers, *The Anti-Federalist Papers* – Anti-Federalist No. 23 ,Taken from the 8th essay of "Brutus" in the *New York Journal*, Jan 10, 1788.

not—exceed the number of citizens willing or able to pay taxes to cover the benefits;

- because the manipulative hand of the government, and not the invisible hand of the natural marketplace, is responsible for the rise in stock market prices;

- because the government has developed a professional volunteer military instead of a drafted military in order to segregate or dampen the citizens' political involvement in evaluating military actions;

- because older generations and their governing representatives discount the lives of future generations by urging or condoning increases in the national debt.

All of these causes of change have their roots embedded in the power of unlimited government borrowing.

It is an inevitable fact that this nation will experience hyperinflation, be forced to declare bankruptcy, or both, because of unlimited government borrowing. The debt we owe as a nation has the power to destroy the domestic tranquility we have been taking for granted for so long. It has the power to extinguish both the common defense and the general welfare of citizens, as well as suffocate justice. This great burden of responsibility for the debt unquestionably falls on all citizens—after all, what is a democratic republic about if not responsibility? Therefore, it is imperative that citizens persuade their state governors and legislators to amend the Constitution.

Only through constitutional amendment processes (some of which will have to be reinvented) can changes be made that have any chance of keeping the Union together. (Ironically, citizens who successfully try to preserve the familiar and comfortable operations of the current

government will end up causing greater, uncontrolled change. The result will end up being worse.)

The states have not had a Constitutional Convention since the beginning of the nation. In fact, they do not know how to have one. This gap in experience should not hinder the responsibility of self-rule. The states must adopt measures to allow a convention to be held, and if need be, without the two national parties' authorization. The importance of this is stated in the following quote:

A QUOTE FOR THE LEADERS OF THE INDIVIDUAL STATES:
"The preservation of the states in a certain degree of agency is indispensable," stated John Dickinson, the Delaware delegate at the 1787 Constitutional Convention, "It will produce the collision between the different authorities that should be wished for in order to check each other."[9]

The following proposed amendments are meant to begin the process of serious change. These amendments decrease the responsibility and power of the central government, and increase the responsibility and power of the states and citizens, while at the same time preserving the Union of 50 states.

The proposed New Age Amendments would augment the current Constitution by imposing sorely needed

---

[9] Bonner, William and Wiggin, Addison. *The Rise and Fall of an Epic Financial Bubble - The new Empire of Debt.* (John Wiley & Sons, Inc., 2009) p. 130.

checks and balances to: government finances, the use of a
professional volunteer military, the control of creating and
dispersing government benefits, the influences of Wall Street,
and the obligation of preserving the freedom and prosperity
for future generations of citizens.

Let this list of New Age Amendments motivate the
states to overcome political inertia by encouraging
assertiveness and boosting responsibility for what happens in
Washington, DC. This will allow for civil and peaceful
change. Thus, in order to form a more perfect union, state
legislatures should begin the vital process of changing the
Constitution with all due velocity.

INDEX OF NEW AGE CONSTITUTIONAL AMENDMENTS

1. MANDATORY CONSTITUTIONAL CONVENTIONS

2. DISCRETIONARY CONSTITUTIONAL CONVENTIONS

3. SUBMISSION OF AMENDMENTS BY THE SUPREME COURT

4. ELECTORAL COLLEGE CHANGE

5. REMOVAL OF CONGRESSIONAL BORROWING

6. THE FINANCIAL BRANCH

7. AD HOC - THE COMMERCE BRANCH

8. THE ENTERPRISE BRANCH

9. BENEFITS OF FINANCIALLY RESPONSIBLE STATES

10. RESTRICT NATIONAL MINIMUM WAGE INCREASES

11. ONE SUBJECT FOR EACH BILL

12. ELIMINATE LANGUAGE ABUSE ON BILLS

13. LINE ITEM VETO

14. A FAIR AND SIMPLIFIED TAX CODE

15. TERM LIMITS FOR THE LEGISLATIVE BRANCH

16. DISSEMINATION OF GOVERNMENT FINANCIAL STATEMENTS

17. FINANCIAL REPORT TO THE UNION

18. LOBBYING RESTRICTIONS OF COMPANIES

19. LOBBYING RESTRICTIONS OF FORMER CONGRESSMEN AND PRESIDENTS

20. LOBBYING RESTRICTIONS OF GOVERNMENT EMPLOYEES

21. SEPARATION OF WALL STREET AND STATE

22. RESTRICTIONS OF OWNERSHIP OF SECURITIES

23. BILL LENGTH AND TIME EXTENSIONS

24. APPROVAL OF EXPENDITURES USING LOCAL MONIES

25. SUBMISSION OF A BALANCE OR SURPLUS BUDGET

26. PRIVATE BUSINESS RESCUE

27. PROLONG BUDGE DEFICITS

28. ILLEGAL IMMIGRATION

29. REVIEW OF THE HOUSE OF REPRESENTATIVES

30. REVIEW OF THE SENATE

31. SHUTDOWN CAUSE AND EFFECT

32. PROTECTION FROM GOVERNMENT SHUTDOWNS

Other Recommended Amendments to the Constitution:

1

1. ## MANDATORY CONSTITUTIONAL CONVENTIONS:

A mandatory Constitutional Convention shall take place every 20 years from when the last mandatory convention took place. The first mandatory convention will take place one year after this amendment has been ratified by the states.

   a. There will not be any participation of any present or former congressmen, presidents, or Supreme Court justices.

2. ## DISCRETIONARY CONSTITUTIONAL CONVENTIONS:

The states, whenever they deem it necessary, can call for a Constitutional Convention on any issue having to do with the ethics, codes of conduct, rules, laws, and benefits relating to the operation of, the members of, or the former members of the executive and the legislative branches.

   a. The Constitutional Convention can be held without petitioning Congress.
   b. Once a date and the location of the convention are established, Congress must be notified.
   c. Once the considered amendment(s) has been passed by 75% of the convention's representatives, the amendment(s) will then be delivered to the states for ratification.
   d. States will have four (4) years to ratify the amendment(s).
   e. As soon as 75% of the states ratify the amendment(s), it becomes part of the Constitution.

3. ## SUBMISSION OF AMENDMENTS BY THE SUPREME COURT:

The Supreme Court can submit, directly to the states, one amendment to the Constitution once every 10

years.
a. The amendment must be approved unanimously by the members of the court.
b. The amendment must be ratified by 75% of the states within two (2) years.
c. Individual state law will dictate whether the people of the state, or the state legislatures, will vote on the amendment.

4. **<u>ELECTORAL COLLEGE CHANGE:</u>**
   For presidential elections, if the nation has trade deficits or financial deficits three out of the last four prior years, the states, and Electoral College, will adhere to these sets of rules:
   a. No state can enact a "winner-take-all" system. All states must allow for the splitting of electoral votes.
   b. No state law can disallow or require a pledge of an elector to vote for the person who won the popular vote in the state.
   c. Political parties cannot obligate or require electors to pledge to vote based on popular vote or for a certain party.
   d. The winner must have at least 30% of the votes.
   e. If no candidate receives 30% of electoral votes, the governors of the states shall vote for one of the five presidential candidates that received the highest populous vote.
   f. If there is a tie of Electoral College votes between candidates, the governors of the states shall decide who will be president.
      i. If there is a tie in the governors' vote, the House of Representatives will decide who the next president will be.

5. **REMOVAL OF CONGRESSIONAL BORROWING:**
Congress shall no longer have the power to borrow money.

6. **THE FINANCIAL BRANCH:**
A fourth branch of government called the Financial Branch shall be created.

   a. The Financial Branch shall have the power to borrow money in the name of the people. No other branch shall have this power.

   b. Congress, when it needs extra funds above and beyond what they are willing to collect in the form of taxation, must submit a request to the Financial Branch explaining how they will spend the money. The Financial Branch can impose qualifications and require restrictions on how the borrowed money is to be spent and paid back. Congress would have the duty to follow the word and spirit of terms laid out by the Financial Branch of government.

   c. The Financial Branch shall dictate pay, health benefits, bonuses, and other benefits of congressmen.

      i. Bonuses can and should be paid only in the event of three consecutive years of federal budget surpluses. The bonuses can be retroactive.

      ii. The pay and benefits of congressmen should be docked if they do not adhere to the Financial Branch's terms placed on any barrowed money given to Congress.

   d. The Financial Branch is to review all bills prior to being sent to the president for his signature. The branch shall have the power of line item veto on all parts of the bill that do not relate to the main subject or title of the bill. *[This will take affect if the*

"Line Item Veto" amendment is not ratified by the states.]

e. The Financial Branch is to be responsible for constructing and implementing strategies and payment schedules to first pay down the foreign debt, and second, pay down the debt owed to the citizens.

f. The Financial Branch shall have the power to audit the finances of any part of the government, including the military and other branches of government.

   i. They have the power to create financial rules and establish criminal penalties if the financial rules are broken or audits are hindered.

g. The Financial Branch must approve all forms of foreign aid when a budget deficit existed the prior year, or a deficit is run up during the previous two (2) quarters of the current year.

h. The Financial Branch shall have the power to set a tax on imported oil and gas. They may also proxy Congress to set the tax rate.

i. Congress must get the approval of the Financial Branch when making loan guarantees for any reason if a trade deficit exists for either of the previous two (2) years.

j. The Financial Branch can pay bonuses to members of the newly formed Enterprise Branch and Commerce Branch of government if they acquire surpluses for the taxpayers. *[This will take affect if the "Enterprise Branch" and the "Ad Hoc-The Commerce Branch" amendments are ratified by the states.]*

k. The Financial Branch will regulate the Federal Reserve with respect to printing of money and auditing any and all financial decisions and transactions, and may impose criminal penalties for hindering audits or for violation of regulations.

l. A security force can be used to enforce regulations and penalties.

m. The Financial Branch shall be made up of a single representative selected by each of the states' legislatures, from all states that have balanced their state budgets during the previous two (2) years.

   i. If less than 60% of the states satisfy this requirement, the states with the least amount of deficit per capita during the two (2) previous years will be allowed to be represented. In this case, the number of states represented cannot exceed 60% of the number of states.

n. The representative must have never held a national political office, worked in a federal job, worked for a federally contracted company or been hired by the national government. The age of the representative must be between the ages of 24 and 40. There shall be a 3-year term limit.

7. **<u>AD HOC - THE COMMERCE BRANCH</u>**
   If trade deficits exist for three consecutive years, a fifth branch of government will come into existence, the Commerce Branch.

   a. The Commerce Branch shall be made up of one representative from each state who is appointed by the governor of each state, and will be paid by the state from which they came, and may serve no more than four (4) years.

   b. The Commerce Branch shall remain active until there are two (2) consecutive years of trade surpluses.

      i. The Commerce Branch shall have the power to review and revoke previously adopted trade agreements created by Congress.

      ii. The Commerce Branch shall have the power

to create new trade agreements with foreign
countries on behalf of the United States.

   iii. During the period of time that the Commerce
Branch is active, Congress will have no power
to create or rescind trade agreements, or set
or reduce tariffs on imports.

   iv. The Commerce Branch shall possess power
to lower the minimum wage, and set tariffs on
imported goods and services.

8. **THE ENTERPRISE BRANCH:**

A sixth branch of government, the Enterprise
Branch, will be newly created. It shall be responsible
for creating government business entities that secure
profit in the name of the taxpayer, thus reducing the
importation and reliance on foreign goods and
services. The secondary goal of the Enterprise Branch
will be to strive to make the country energy
independent while maintaining reasonable ecological
standards.

a. This branch shall be comprised of one appointee
from each state, each serving one 6-year term. A
state may replace or call back their representative
at any time.

b. The branch shall act as a board of directors, or
will elect or appoint board members for any
business entity they create or head.

c. Eighty percent of all profits created by the
Enterprise Branch will be turned over to the
Financial Branch of government. The remaining
twenty percent would remain in an account of the
Enterprise Branch as seed money for special
business investment projects.

*[If the Financial Branch amendment is not ratified by the
states, then seventy percent of all profits will be turned over to
Congress, and thirty percent will remain in an account of the
Enterprise Branch as seed money for special business*

investment projects.]

9. BENEFITS OF FINANCIALLY RESPONSIBLE STATES:

Only congressmen from states that balance their budgets during the previous two (2) years are allowed to vote on federal budget bills and budget resolutions.

a. At least 60% of the states must be allowed to vote on budget bills and resolutions. If fewer than 60% of the states qualify, those with the lowest debt per capita will be allowed to vote. The number of states is not to exceed 60% in this case.

b. The U.S. Senate will dictate the uniform accounting rules that states need to follow in order to qualify.

10. RESTRICT NATIONAL MINIMUM WAGE INCREASES:

Congress is disallowed from increasing the national minimum wage if the national trade balance is negative in any of the previous three (3) years.

11. ONE SUBJECT PER BILL

No bill, except general appropriation bills, shall be passed containing more than one subject, which shall be clearly expressed in its title; but if any subject shall be embraced in any act which shall not be expressed in the title, such act shall be void only as to so much thereof as shall not be so expressed.[10]

---

[10] Constitution of the State of Colorado, Article V-:egislative Department, Section 21. Bill to contain but one subject - expressed in title. Office of Legislative Legal Services, Dan L. Cartin, Director 04/17/15, http://tornado.state.co.us/gov_dir/leg_dir/olls/constitution.htm#ARTICLE_V_S ection_21

12. <u>ELIMINATE LANGUAGE ABUSE ON BILLS</u>:

All bills must be written in plain English so as not to deliberately deceive other members of any branch of government or the people, or to deliberately hide the meaning of any part of the legislation.[11] Misuse of language, use of code, use of non-common lexicon shall cause the article to be automatically voided.

a. The Senate has the duty to ensure that all bills can easily be read and understood in the language of the nation.

b. The president shall have the power and the duty to void articles in bills that are not interpretable by the common citizen.

c. The voided articles shall then go back to the Senate, who will then have 10 days to clarify the language.

d. Any disputes on language will be sent to the Financial Branch of government for review. If the Fourth Branch does not approve the language with a 50% vote, the article is void.

[If the Financial Branch amendment is not ratified, the governors of the states will rule on the disputes.]

13. <u>LINE ITEM VETO</u>:

A 3-person committee from the senate shall have the power of line item veto.

a. The 3-member committee will be made up of senators from the states that have the greatest budget surpluses per capita (or least deficits per capita).

b. The term the senators will serve on the committee will be one (1) year.

c. Once a state has been represented on the committee, it cannot be represented again for the

---

[11] Prompted by Jack Abramoff's interview on CBS's 60 Minutes.

next two (2) years.

d. Each individual vetoed line item can be overridden by Congress with a majority vote of more than 60%.

e. The vetoed line items must be voted upon individually and not as a group.

14. A FAIR AND SIMPLIFIED TAX CODE:

Congress must fashion a progressive, flat tax standard. Congress can only apply up to six tax deductions to the tax laws and no more.

a. Each deduction must be specific and clear to all common citizens.

b. Once Congress decides what deductions to set into the tax code, each of the deductions must be approved by the Senate before becoming law.

c. Any changes to the deductions must be approved by the Senate.

d. Congress must provide or make available a free computer program for all citizens to use to calculate accurately the minimal amount of tax the citizen owes, thus eliminating the need for citizens to have tax consultants.

e. Citizens who do not pay a minimum tax of 10% of their earnings will be disqualified from voting in the next congressional election.

15. TERM LIMITS FOR THE LEGISLATIVE BRANCH

There shall be a 2-term limit for members of the House of Representatives and for members of the Senate.

a. Congressmen can exceed the 2-term limit if 65% of the Financial Branch of government approves of them running again. In this case, there is no limit to how many times they can run for office.

[If the Financial Branch amendment is not ratified by

the states, the terms *of office cannot be extended.]*

16. <u>**DISSEMINATION OF GOVERNMENT FINANCIAL STATEMENTS:**</u>

Congress must deliver to each registered voter an annual summary of the nation's financial statement, including a balance sheet of the government's finances at the end of every fiscal year.

a. The summary shall be eight pages in length and can be delivered in the form of a hard copy or electronic copy—choice of the voter.

b. The first page of the summary must list:
   iii. The amount of the national debt(in numeric format);
   iv. The names of the top three foreign countries that hold US debt and their amounts;
   v. The voter's home state's share of the national debt;
   vi. The voter's share of the national debt. This is to be figured by taking the number of people over the age of 18 in the country minus the number of unemployed and dividing that number into the national debt.
   vii. The voter's share of the national debt for each of the previous 10 years;
   viii. The voter's projected share of the national debt for 1 year, 5 years and 10 years into the future based on the current statistical trend.

17. <u>**FINANCIAL REPORT TO THE UNION:**</u>

Prior to the president's State of the Union address, the Office of Management and Budget (OMB) shall deliver the "State of the Finances" speech—a half-hour to one-hour long presentation on the state of the United States' true finances for that year, and the overall finances of the United States. This will include the trend of the nation's financial situation and trade

balance.

a. The president and Congress shall not influence what is presented in any way.

b. Entities that broadcast or display the State of the Union speech must also broadcast or display the "State of the Finances" speech.

18. LOBBYING RESTRICTIONS OF COMPANIES:

No multinational company can lobby Congress nor support organizations that lobby Congress, nor can they contribute to a congressman's campaigns, foundations, or to his party unless they have paid at least 5% of their profits in taxes.

a. No domestic company can lobby Congress nor support organizations that lobby Congress, nor contribute to a congressman's campaigns, foundations, or his political party unless they have at least paid 4% of their profits in taxes.

b. No company that is foreign-owned can lobby Congress nor support organizations that lobby Congress, nor can they contribute to the campaigns, foundations, or political parties of anyone running for the positions of congressman or president.

c. Accepting significant foreign money can be interpreted by the courts as a treasonable act, thereby could apply punishments commensurate with the crime.

19. LOBBYING RESTRICTIONS OF FORMER CONGRESSMEN AND PRESIDENTS:

All former congressmen and presidents, and their staffs, shall be disallowed to lobby congressmen or the presiding president, or work for or contract with

any company that lobbies or seeks a federal government contract or seeks congressional favors.[12]

   a. Former congressmen and presidents and immediate family cannot work for or contract with any foreign nation, nor accept money or significant gifts.

   b. Accepting significant foreign money can be interpreted by the courts as a treasonable act, thereby could apply punishments commensurate with the crime.

20. LOBBYING RESTRICTIONS OF GOVERNMENT EMPLOYEES:

All present and former US government employees shall be disallowed to lobby Congress for private and foreign businesses.

21. SEPARATION OF WALL STREET AND STATE:

No Wall Street firm (financial firms that deal with the buying and selling of stocks and bonds) can lobby Congress or support organizations that lobby Congress.

   a. No member of Wall Street firms' boards of directors, officers within the firms, or anyone representing those firms can contribute to the campaigns or foundations of congressmen or presidential candidates.

   b. No one who has been hired by these firms can be appointed as chairman of the Federal Reserve.

---

[12] A similar suggestion was recommended by Jack Abramoff in a CBS *60 Minutes* interview.

22. RESTRICTIONS OF OWNERSHIP OF SECURITIES:

During the period that congressmen and the president and their staffs are in office and for one (1) year following, they and their immediate families shall be disallowed to buy or sell stocks or bonds.

a. Members of Congress, the president, or federal judges are not protected from and can be charged with insider trading violations.

b. This amendment can be retroactively applied.

23. BILL LENGTH AND TIME EXTENSIONS:

For congressional bills with more than 300 pages, the president will have an additional day for each 100 additional pages over the 300 pages to veto or sign the bill.

a. For congressional bills with more than 750 pages, the president will have an additional day for every 30 additional pages over the 750 pages to either sign the bill, veto the bill, or do nothing.

b. For bills over 750 pages, if the president neither vetoes nor signs it, the bill will be vetoed automatically at the end of the time period.

c. All bills over 750 pages that are signed by the president will be returned to Congress. Congress must then pass the bill once more, with absolutely no change to its contents, between 7 and 25 days after the bill is returned. Once the bill passes Congress again, it becomes law. If the bill does not pass the second time, it becomes null and void.

24. APPROVAL OF EXPENDITURES USING LOCAL MONIES

Any bill passed by Congress and the president that mandates state or local governments to take action that results in the expenditures of state or local funds

must also be passed by 50% of the Financial Branch of government before it becomes law.

[If the Financial Branch amendment is not ratified by the states, 50% of the governors must pass the bill before it becomes law.]

25. SUBMISSION OF A BALANCED OR SURPLUS BUDGET

The president, as part of his duties, must always submit to Congress a balanced budget or a surplus budget plan for the upcoming fiscal year.

a. If the president does not submit such a budget:

    i. He or she will be prohibited from running for a second term or hold any other federal office.

    ii. The political party of which the president is a member will be ineligible to sponsor a candidate for the office of president for the next election.

    iii. The president's benefits after leaving office will be reduced by 50%.

26. PRIVATE BUSINESS RESCUE

The bailout of any private business entity must be approved by 65% of the Financial Branch.

[If the Financial Branch amendment is not ratified by the states, then 65% of the Congress AND 65% of the governors of the states must approve the bailout.]

a. The bailout can only occur if the Federal Government had accumulated a financial surplus the prior year as reported by the Office of Management and Budget.

b. The Enterprise Branch of government must be given full control of the company that is to be bailed out.

[If the Enterprise Branch amendment is not ratified by the states, Congress shall manage the business entity and make efforts to achieve a substantial profit for the taxpayers.]

27. <u>PROLONGED BUDGET DEFICITS</u>

If budget deficits exist for four straight years,
Congress must submit the budget for the next year
directly to the people for a vote.

    a. If the people disapprove, Congress can submit
one more budget directly to the people.

    b. If the second budget is disapproved, all
congressional representatives will end their term
that year and the people shall elect new
representatives to take their place.

*[This amendment would be contingent on the Financial Branch
amendment not being ratified by the states.]*

28. <u>ILLEGAL IMMIGRATION</u>

    a. State and local law enforcement shall have the
right to enforce all federal laws concerning illegal
immigration, including the deportation of such
individuals.

    b. The states also can take action to prevent illegal
immigration into their state, including the posting
of guards at the border and building walls.

    c. States may enact laws that will make it unlawful
for illegal immigrants to receive any state or
national services, vote, or become a state resident.
This would trump any federal law.

    d. The cost of deportation must be paid by the
federal government to the states.

29. <u>REVIEW OF THE HOUSE OF REPRESENTATIVES</u>

Every ten years, the citizens will vote in approval or
disapproval of the performance of the House of
Representatives as a whole. If 75% of the voters
disapprove of the performance, all members of the
House must be replaced with new members the
following year.

a. No displaced congressional member can run again for his/her seat or any other seat.
b. For a new member of House of Representatives who had been elected the same year that this vote is taken, he/she would retain his/her newly elected position for the full term.

[This amendment would be contingent on the Term Limits amendment not being ratified by the states.]

30. <u>REVIEW OF THE SENATE</u>

Every ten years, the citizens will vote on their general approval or disapproval of the performance of the Senate as a whole. If 70% of the voters disapprove of the performance of the Senate, the entire Senate must be replaced with new members within two (2) years.
a. No displaced Senator can run again for his/her seat or any other seat.
b. For a new member of the Senate who is elected the same or prior year that the vote is taken, he/she would retain his/her newly elected position for the full term.

[This amendment would be contingent on the Term Limits amendment not being ratified by the states.]

31. <u>SHUTDOWN CAUSE AND EFFECT</u>

If the government's lack of funds results in a government shutdown, government employees that are put on furlough will not receive back pay or any future compensation for the time the government is shut down.

32. <u>PROTECTION FROM GOVERNMENT SHUTDOWNS</u>

During government shutdowns, any government department whose total cost of doing business is less than the amount of money that department brings into the government (that is, the department creates a surplus for the taxpayer), shall not be furloughed during government shutdowns.

33. <u>CITIZENS' CONFLICT OF INTEREST REDUCED:</u>

If what a citizen directly receives from the government in benefits (Social Security, food stamps, health care, etc.) exceeds what that citizen had contributed to the government in taxes thus far in life, that citizen will be disallowed to vote for congressmen during the election years in which he/she receives benefits, and one election year after the cessation of benefits.

a. For citizens who have declared bankruptcy and are financially relieved from the debt via taxpayer bailout or other form of government program that is paid for by taxpayers…
   i. That citizen will be disallowed to vote for congressmen until the amount of debt is paid back in full.
   ii. That citizen's future government benefits can be docked in order to recover some or all of the money owed.

34. <u>REDUCE MILITARY CONFLICT OF INTEREST:</u>

If at least one-third of the total number of soldiers in a branch of the military is made up of non-drafted soldiers, all those non-drafted soldiers within that branch shall be disallowed to vote for congressmen during the time periods of non-declared wars.

35. **CHECK AND BALANCE USE OF MILITARY:**
When more than 50% of a military branch is made up
of non-drafted soldiers, an approval vote of 50% of
the state's governors is needed to use these
professional volunteer troops and any military
equipment on foreign soil.
   a. Governors shall not have a say in the use of
      drafted personnel.
   b. Governors can give their power of vote to a
      proxy.

36. **FOREIGN CONTRIBUTIONS TO
GOVERNMENT OFFICIALS OR THEIR
FAMILIES**
National government officials, their immediate
families, foundations, or any other related entity must
report all accepted or promised monies and
contributions from foreign entities to the US
government and to the state in which the officials
reside. That information is to be made available to the
public.
   a. Any acceptance of significant foreign
      contributions will automatically trigger an
      investigation through either the national attorney
      or the state attorney or both, for the purpose of
      deciding whether the accepting of monies and
      gifts constitutes a high crime and misdemeanors.
   b. The state attorney can act independently from the
      national attorney and can level charges against the
      involved official and immediate family members.
   c. Accepting significant foreign money can be
      interpreted by the courts as a treasonable act.
      Punishments commensurate with the crime could
      be applied.

37. <u>FINANCIAL RESPONSIBILITY OF SECEDING STATES</u>

For any state to secede from the Union, the state and its people must agree to take full responsibility for their share of the Union's foreign debt (figured per capita) and their share of the domestic debt.

Other Recommended Amendments to the Constitution:

38. TERM LIMITS FOR THE JUDICIAL BRANCH:

Term limits for the members of the Supreme Court shall be 30 years, or until they have reached the age of 70, whichever comes first.

39. STATES' CONTROL OF SUPREME COURT RULINGS

If a Supreme Court decision on a case yields a one-vote difference between the sides, the court must vote on it again within two (2) months.

a. If the decision still has a one-vote difference, the states' legislatures have two (2) years to vote whether or not to allow the case to become an individual state's issue.

b. If 75% of the states' legislatures vote for state control on the issue, the Supreme Court ruling itself would become void, and each individual state would be left to decide the issue.

40. PROTECTION FOR PRIVATELY HELD PRECIOUS METALS:

Government shall make no law restricting or reducing the private ownership of gold and silver (coin or bullion) by citizens.

a. Local, state, and federal governments shall not have the power to confiscate gold and silver coin or bullion from law-abiding, private citizens.

b. The Federal Government shall not have the power to confiscate gold and silver coin or bullion from local governments or states.

c. The Federal Government can reasonably tax the

raw gold and silver found or mined by mining
companies and individual prospectors.

41. **<u>PENALTY FOR SOCIAL PROGRAM FRAUD</u>:**
Individuals or companies that knowingly cheat and
defraud government social programs (Social Security,
Medicaid, food stamps, etc.) or act to separate
citizens from their government benefits by fraudulent
means, can be tried for treason when considered
reasonable. Extraordinary penalties can be handed
down for such fraud when reasonable.

42. **EXAM FOR CONGRESSMEN**
Prior to taking their positions in the House of
Representatives or the Senate, all members must pass
an exam contain information on the principles of
freedom, the Federalist and Anti-Federalist papers,
ethics and virtues related to governing and freedom,
and human nature's propensities to undermine
freedom.

43. **<u>PROOF OF CITIZENSHIP TO VOTE</u>:**
Only citizens of the United States have a privilege to
vote in the country's national elections. In order for
citizens to participate in this privilege, they can be
required to prove their citizenship.

44. <u>POST-AMBLE TO THE CONSTITUTION – RESPONSIBILITIES OF CITIZENS</u>

For the mutual and general welfare of the nation, citizens of this Union need to perform these duties to the best of their abilities:

- Be responsible for paying back personal debts.
- Bear the burden of the financial debts of their nation.
- Bear the burden of their national representatives' actions.
- Be responsible for personal happiness without injury to others.
- Be responsible for personal health and health care.
- Be responsible for personal investments, education, and retirement.
- Be respectful of those with differing points of view.
- Ensure the government treats all citizens equally.
- Have civility and promote calmness.

❧

❧

1   *I*ndebtedness was NOT an original founding
2   principle on which the Union was built, nor was it the reason
3   the Union survived for more than 200 years. Though the *New*
4   *Age Amendments* may at first seem undesirable, disagreeable,
5   and unimaginable, one must give the idea of new
6   amendments serious consideration when acknowledging
7   these factors: 1) The nation's uncontrollably growing deficits
8   exceed a trillion dollars. 2) The country's unending spewing
9   of trade deficits now tally more than nine trillion dollars. 3)
10 Debt has a historical characteristic of causing disorder,
11 instability, and anarchy in societies.
12   The fact is that the money has been borrowed and
13 the money has been spent, recklessly and without proper
14 thought, in many different ways and for many different
15 reasons in a wide range of forms and programs: social
16 programs and charities, military actions, outer space projects,
17 economic stimulus, and education. The importance of these
18 programs does not justify our government to spend freely,
19 thoughtlessly, or without proper strategic planning. The two
20 parties' reckless financial mind-sets are leading the nation into
21 a constitutional crisis that can only be avoided by altering the
22 Constitution. Framing the situation in this light gives the *New*
23 *Age Amendments* immediate significance.
24   Stepping back, it seems suitable while considering
25 such enormous changes—changes that require the
26 application of wisdom—to consider one of the many
27 definitions of wisdom:

> *Wisdom is a deep understanding and realization of people, things, events, or situations, resulting in the ability to apply perceptions, judgments, and actions. In keeping with this understanding, it often requires control of one's emotional reactions (the passions) so that universal principles, reason, and knowledge prevail.*[13]

The Constitution was intended to be made more perfect through the amendment process. With the progression of time, a change in attitude, and the increase in the nation's population, the prescribed process in Article 5 of the present Constitution has become obsolete. Perhaps it was never usable in the first place. In the face of the national financial difficulties we have allowed to develop over recent decades, we must acknowledge the failure of Article 5. Now, we must apply vast amounts of wisdom to engineer a different and better way to amend and improve the Constitution.

Improving the Constitution will require discussing, cultivating, creating, refining, and enhancing the *New Age Amendments*. This process should begin as soon as possible, for when the elasticity of the nation's indebtedness reaches the point of failure—when the financial rubber band breaks—the snap will cause great disorientation of the people. This disorientation, along with the intensification of emotions, will make it much more difficult for the people to render proper changes to the Constitution. It is easier to fix a

---

[13] From a previous version of a Wikipedia article on Wisdom.

1   boat in calm waters than in stormy seas.

2   As we apply wisdom with proper action, let our
3   discussions concerning the creation and adoption of new
4   amendments not rip apart our bonds of shared culture,
5   common history, and national identity. Let the process
6   increase our virtues in a way that all of humankind can look
7   to us as a great example of self-rule.

8   Despite differing opinions about what should be
9   done on the rough and tortuous road ahead, it is in our best
10 interest, and in the interest of our younger generation, to
11 cooperate with each other, but not compromise on what is
12 needed to fix the financial problems of the nation. For
13 proper change to happen, we must be prepared to make great
14 sacrifices.

15   We the people of this democratic society, this
16 republic, are meant to be responsible for the government.
17 There is no one else.

Part 3.
Grievances Against the Citizens of the United States

> *...We must not let our rulers load us with perpetual debt. We must make our election between economy and liberty or profusion and servitude.*[14]
> — *Thomas* Jefferson

✧

> *If destruction be our lot we must ourselves be its author and finisher. As a nation of freemen we must live through all time or die by suicide.*[15]
> —Abraham Lincoln

✧

𝔚e, the citizens of the United States, have voted to trade past years of being "better off" in exchange for future years of financial agony—the financial agony of having to pay back the astronomical amounts of money borrowed to make the better off years possible. We have rejected thrift and future freedom, and instead elected current abundance and future slavery—exactly what Thomas Jefferson condemned.

We, the citizens of the United States, have kept quiet about the question of supporting a government whose financial system cannot go on in its present form—a system that generates debt instead of earning surpluses. We have

[14] Jefferson, Thomas. *The Works of Thomas Jefferson, vol. 12 (Correspondence and Papers 1816-1826)* [1905] http://oll.libertyfund.org/titles/808
[15] Lincoln, Abraham. *Speeches and Letters of Abraham Lincoln*, The Project Gutenberg eBook, 1832-1865, Edited by Merwin Roe, www.gutenberg.net Release Date: January 17, 2005 [eBook #14721].

been effortlessly seduced by promises of all kinds of benefits and money—retirement, health care, unemployment checks, a good economy, etc.—by the political parties. These tainted awards cause us to fail to apply the principles we know about personal finance to the finances of our central government. Over the last 35 years, we have been dissolving the great political and economic advantages that this country has had over all other countries of the world. The amount of debt we have vs. the amount of debt we the citizens are able and willing to make payments on is tremendously out of equilibrium. Unimaginable oppression waits in the wings as the nature of finance readies to move toward balance. The nature of finance has no heart or tolerance for men and women of countries who ignore her unwavering laws concerning surpluses and deficits.

It is essential for the citizens to know the part they have played in forming the coming economic and political consequences caused by the past financial decisions of our chosen representatives. It is important for the citizens to understand their own past and current habitual mind-sets, which will lead to unwanted changes in our society and country. Only through understanding and recognition of our human nature's tendency to simply and stealthily be seduced by money can past mistakes be purposefully rectified. The "Grievances against the Citizens of the United States" are here not to accuse, but to help all of us recognize within ourselves some of our human frailties as a basis to make corrections to the Constitution, to the course our country is on, and to our own attitudes and beliefs.

For your deep analysis and discussion, here are the grievances against the citizens of the United States:

Grievances against Citizens who are Leaders of Religious Organizations

"Thou shall not steal" is a basic decree of religion. You, leaders of American religious organizations, have remained quiet while our national government has been stealing from the children of the future for more than 35 years. The United States government is borrowing exorbitant sums of money without any intention of paying it back. This is stealing on a scale unseen in human history. You American religious leaders have not given the national debt a moral review or voiced objections. This silence is condoning and giving your absolute blessing on this sin. Your silence is helping to induce widespread future suffering of your parishioners and their children.

You must morally review the financial conduct of the US government and speak up about this evil.

As a note to the principle of separation of church and state, when the state goes bankrupt, only the church remains standing. It will be the church that will provide civility, stability, and order to our society in the absence of a trustworthy central government. You religious leaders must prepare yourselves and your churches for the coming changes.

Grievances against Citizens who work with Accounts Payable, Accounts Receivable, and General Ledgers, and those who are CFOs

You citizens absolutely know that, in the businesses where you work, receivables must exceed payables, else those businesses you work for will cease to exist and you will be out of a job. Yet, for decades, you have not applied this knowledge when evaluating your government's financial situation. You have remained quiet concerning the condition of the payables and receivables of the government.

In addition, you have said nothing about the rogue accounting practices that the two parties use to mislead the citizens into thinking the finances of the government are well run.

You need to support and vote for members of Congress who are financially responsible and will fight for the use of accurate accounting practices throughout the government complex. You need to convince other citizens who do not have your understanding to look for and vote for fiscally responsible representatives. At this point in our history, of all the election issues, it is fiscal responsibility (and the virtues of integrity and foresight) that must be put far above any other issue or reason for voting for a candidate. For our liberty and the government to continue to exist, the government must start amassing consistent yearly surpluses to pay down the debt.

Grievances against Teachers and Professors

Your educational institutions should give citizens the knowledge to keep from being seduced by unwise government spending. But your own education does not even protect you from being blinded by the money the government dispenses.

From local public school systems up to the highest educational institutions—Yale, Berkeley, Harvard, and MIT—all of you have failed the country in this way. You have failed to recognize the human instinct that allows your own financial seduction to take place. Furthermore, you have failed to educate your students on the seductive power of money, particularly and especially the harm to liberty that occurs when that money is borrowed and dispensed by the central government. The proof of the failing of the education system is the ratio between the unimaginable amount of national debt and the minuscule outcry of the citizens against that debt.

You need to rethink and reinvent curricula that will enable citizens to defend themselves against the seduction of money, and help them understand the importance of keeping the Federal Government finances balanced. (Uncontrolled debt is something that the Founding Fathers warned us could erase freedom.) New curricula should include information on the ways democracies destroy themselves financially. This would enable citizens to be vigilant for warning signs that their freedoms are under attack. Your new curricula need to plant and establish new methods and patterns of thinking that will allow the principles of freedom to live within the minds of citizens. This must happen from the lowest to the very highest levels of our educational structure.

Grievances against Citizens who Vote based on wanting Lower Taxes

For decades, you have supported and voted for candidates from both major political parties who will not raise taxes "today." Yet these same representatives spend astronomical amounts of money in excess of tax receipts. This utterly undercuts your goal to continue to have lower taxes in the future. It is also counterproductive to vote for candidates who have enacted policies that help create trade deficits, as these deficits lead to increased tax burdens.

The vast majority of citizens would agree that your goal to lower taxes is grand; it is very popular. However, your strategy has not only been counterproductive to your goal, but also destructive to the country.

Debt is a tax that is hidden; it is revealed only when it is too late to take action against it. It is the titanic amount of debt that produces poverty and rebellion. (Are we going to rebel because of our own past decisions?) With this situation, we have inflicted upon ourselves an increase in future taxes. The taxes that will have to come will be overwhelming. There are no extrications or bailouts. There will be no release from the responsibility, no relief from repaying, no relaxing of the penalties of the accumulating debt. Sweeping tax increases, conventional and/or through hyperinflation, will have to come.

A related question is, how do the taxpayers pay back the citizens who lent the government money through the purchase of Treasury Bills and US Savings bonds if not through raising taxes? Perhaps this is not obvious; the more debt there is, the less chance those citizens will get their money back.

Understand, the causes of our astronomical debt can

be attributed to corruption running rampant within the governmental structure. This edifice of corruption has been set up and sustained by the leaders of the country—namely the Democratic and Republican parties. Astronomical debt can also be attributed to long-existing, faulty trade agreements and policies. Again, it is the political leadership in our government that over the decades has let this happen.

The time has come when you need to adopt and support new political parties and representatives that slash government spending and promote trade surpluses, and not those parties and representatives that put the country in debt (unless that debt can yield a financial gain or trade surplus for the nation. [Hint: This cannot be done through acts of war.]). Only when the government has surpluses can taxes truly be lowered. The pathway for that to happen is to implement tough controls on all government spending and to vote for candidates of political parties that, once in office, will create an environment of financial honesty, integrity, and responsibility. Your fellow taxpayers need YOU to steer the country onto these new financial paths.

Grievances against Citizens who are Business Leaders

Many businessmen have said, "If I ran my business like the government, I would be out of business." If this axiom is true, then it must also be true that government should run its business like American businesspeople run their organizations—for profit—or else they go out of business. Yet you executives have supported and contributed to political candidates who have spent enormous amounts of money over budget without that money having been invested wisely.

To be clear, just as in for-profit businesses, all non-profit enterprises need surpluses to continue to exist. The Red Cross, Salvation Army, Goodwill Industries International, and the Catholic Church all need surpluses to exist. The US government is a non-profit entity that also needs to acquire surpluses to continue to exist. Governments have become unstable and have lost the trust of their citizens when they have failed to make profits for their citizens.

You American business leaders have NOT been putting your support behind national representatives who have the philosophy of governmental profit—or at least a pay-as-you-go philosophy. You need to begin to apply what you know about the financial bottom line to government finances, and support representatives who will vote for bills that support a bottom line that shows a surplus for the country.

Because money has already been borrowed and spent, and because the national debt continues to grow at an astronomical rate, sooner or later the government will go bankrupt, the currency will be ruined, and economic activity will be a smidgeon of what it is today; that is the bottom line.

But the country needs your involvement to rebuild

1 and create a new foundation for business growth for future
2 generations. Your country needs you to create and support
3 change that will make the government abide by the bottom
4 line and not destroy the finances of our country with
5 unwarranted debt.

Grievances against Citizens who are Leaders of State and Local Political Parties

Is your state a *state*, or a *colony*? A colony is passive and goes along with central government's actions. A state actively reviews and uses independent intelligence to check and balance the central government.

You citizens in state and local governments who belong to one of the two major national political parties have largely remained silent on the subject of the national government's spending habits. In the Founding Fathers' minds, you are an implicit check and balance against abuses by the central government—a protector of your own citizens from the Federal Government's vices and bad decisions. But you have said and done little to nothing to protect your citizens from the damaging financial decisions the central government has been making during the past decades. In fact, many of you have helped to add to the ugly financial situation of the nation by begging and pleading our bankrupted central government for money and benefits. You too have been easily seduced by the borrowing and printing of tainted money rained on your states by the Federal Government. You have become content, complacent, and overly submissive.

Robert Yates, in *Anti-Federalist 45*, predicted the current relationship between the states' government and national government:

> *The state governments are considered in... [the new constitution] as mere dependencies, existing solely by its toleration, and possessing powers of which they may be deprived whenever the general government is disposed so to do.*[16]

Instead of having the courage to challenge harmful federal actions, you have separated yourselves politically from those actions by saying nothing. You give the excuse, "It is their [the national government's] problem, not ours." This is an avoidance of responsibility, which does not bode well for the future of freedom and self-rule.

The fact is, it *is* your problem—and your citizens' problem. You need to involve yourselves and your legislatures in correcting the national government when its own imbecilities are accepted as the "people's will" and the "national interest." You need to begin to take action and go to a higher level of thinking in order to change the U.S. Constitution so as to allow an increase of ability for states to stop unwise Congressional actions, and stop the bureaucracies' activities that become the seeds for exploitation, corruption, or destruction.

The national debt and trade deficits will be an obstacle to the future well-being and freedom of the residents in your state. Because the two political parties controlling the central government continue to take the country on the road

---

[16] Founding Fathers, The. *The Anti-Federalist Papers*, ReadaClassic.com, Layout and cover copyright 2010. p 166

towards bankruptcy and currency destruction, it becomes clear that eventually you, as state leaders, will be forced to think on your own and use your own ingenuity to find solutions to solve the economic problems of your state.

One positive aspect of this is that your state, and the people of your state, will become stronger and self-reliant. One way in which this is bad is that it dissolves the glue that makes the Union a union. States will potentially become adversaries of other states. This situation needs to be prevented—immediately, without delay.

The goals of the Constitutional Convention should be to reduce the powers of Congress that have been abused, and give those powers—and the power of some checks and balances—to the states, while at the same time preserving the cooperation and relationships between the states. It is you, the state leaders, who have to become a leading force behind fixing the flaws in the central government and the Constitution.

At this juncture, your most important task is to find the wisest man in your state, one who would represent your state in a Constitutional Convention. Consider men who are knowledgeable about *The Federalist Papers*, *The Anti-Federalist Papers*, past and present world governments and their philosophies, as well as human dispositions and proclivities. These men should be able to recognize which principles of liberty and freedom have been broken or weakened over the past decades. With their personal integrity, fatherly foresight, and other virtues in place, they need to have the ability to help renovate and enhance these principles through the use of amendments.

Do not wait—you should start on this task immediately. Go out and find the New Age Founding Father

1 that will represent your state at the convention—for the good
2 of the people of your state and the people of the union of
3 states.

Grievances against Citizens who are Economists

• You have failed to evaluate properly the effect increasing the minimum wage has on the number of jobs lost. You have not taken into account the offsetting effect the Federal Government has when it creates jobs by throwing prodigious amounts of borrowed money into the economy. As the growth of the national debt increases, the unemployment rate should decrease. When the minimum wage increases, jobs should decrease. Anything outside these two postulates dictates the need to find reasons why events are not following these rules. This has not been done.

• You have wrongly and without critical mathematical thought used and encouraged the use of the ratio of the amount of national debt to the gross domestic product to evaluate the amount of debt a nation can safely and feasibly tolerate. You have ignored the fact that our government's deficits have had a substantial influence on temporarily increasing the gross domestic product. This makes the debt seem much less poisonous than it actually is and therefore, diminishes the motivations to act against debt. Since one variable influences the value of the other variable by a great amount, it is an unsuitable ratio to use—especially when trade deficits exist. It is imperative for you to realize that the ratio of the amount of the debt to the trade balance is the appropriate ratio to use when evaluating a nation's debt. After all, at an individual level, it is the amount of personal income that determines whether a person's debt is out of control.

• You have advocated free trade without encouraging any evaluation of whether the trade is advantageous or injurious to the country. This is a critical step in trade—determining whether it is positive (beneficial) or negative (harmful) to the nation. A needs assessment is necessary in order to evaluate

which trade policies—including semi-isolationist or
isolationist trade policies—are best. Yet you economists
wrongly assume that trade will always be positive for entities
on both sides of a trade, even though there are many human
and financial factors that can influence whether trade is
negative or positive. Without proper evaluation, your
assumptions with respect to how free trade affects economic
outcomes are greatly and erroneously skewed toward being
positive; they promote any trade agreements, even bad ones.
These mistaken assumptions are a detriment for creating
future trade agreements that would actually produce a strong,
enduring economy for this country.

• You have thoroughly ignored the long-term, cumulative
effect of trade deficits. You have failed to advertise vigorously
the long-term consequences of this to the ruling parties and
citizens. You have failed to recognize the "economic circle of
death": 1) Citizens buy foreign goods, sending the nation's
currency outside our economic system. 2) The government
borrows or prints money to make up for the loss and
distributes it into the national economy. 3) Citizens buy more
foreign goods, which send more money outside our
economic system. 4) The government borrows and prints
more money. 5) Citizens see the economy has not worsened,
so they continue to buy even more foreign goods, sending
even more money outside the economic system. 6) The
government borrows and prints even more money in order to
sustain the current standard of living.

And thus, the circle continues. Faulty expectations of
the citizens see no problem in the "circle"—but you should.
Death comes to the economy when there is so much money
in circulation that foreign entities begin to reject the currency.
This breaks the circle, causing trade to cease and out-of-

control inflation to occur; the circle becomes a spiral. The result is that the American economy is set up to be a fatal victim of its own making.

You economists should have been vigorously opposing this line of action by the Federal Government—borrowing money to stimulate economy—knowing it would only make the future worse. (The borrowing of money would have to yield a trade surplus in order for it to be a positive influence on the future economy.) You should be advocating some form of a balanced budget amendment to be added to the Constitution to limit the circle from turning into a spiral.

It is these inane philosophies and flummoxed mentalities that encourage the thinking that: (1) any economy can continue to be strong in spite of prodigious trade deficits; and (2) increases in the national debt can be perpetual and therefore can sustain an economy forever. These are two preposterous ideas.

• China has been building a military on the trade surpluses they receive from the United States—ironically and regrettably, a military that will obviously be a fearsome future adversary of ours. Yet you economists have said nothing to our leaders, or more importantly to US citizens, about the relationship between China's trade surplus and its military buildup.

• Our government places strict environmental regulations on businesses in this country. Free trade occurs between the Union's states because they are all under the same environmental regulations (and other laws). Several countries that are our trading partners have very few environmental regulations for businesses. This has put US manufacturing businesses at a disadvantage. This situation does not make trade free or fair, and it hurts our economy by pushing

manufacturers out of the country toward countries where
there are lower costs of production. But you have neither
paid attention to, nor have you acknowledged this hindrance
on genuine free trade. And therefore, you have not offered
any solutions to our leaders that would mitigate this
imbalance and allow for the possibility of acquiring trade
surpluses for this country. (A serious solution would be that
we do not allow products from other countries to come into
this country unless those countries have enacted the same
binding environmental laws—and labor laws—that are
imposed on our states. That would then be fair and free
trade.)

• You have ignored the fact that the "invisible hand of the
marketplace" has been replaced by the "manipulative hand of
the government," seriously causing you to misevaluate how
much economic danger the US economy is in.

• You have failed to acknowledge that the upkeep of
government and its programs are an expense on the
economy.

• Regretfully, you have also been seduced by the money our
political leaders are throwing into the economy, making you
content, complacent, and not wanting to rock the economic
boat.

To help this country, you must evaluate these topics
fully, with mathematical logic and without emotion. You
must reevaluate your evaluations. When something
contradicts logic, you must dig deeply into evaluating the
cause of the contradiction instead of just writing it off as
"that is just the way it works." The accuracy of your
economic evaluations must encompass elements of principled
financial law in order to steer our leaders toward decisions
that, in the long-term, will preserve our freedoms and

liberties. Federalist Papers #11 and #12 by Alexander
Hamilton can be used as guidance. This county needs you to
help change its ruinous, long-term economic course into one
of economic stability, even if that means sacrificing current
economic activity.

Grievances against Retired Citizens

Through the years of your adulthood, you have permitted the US government to build destructive deficits. In that period, you refused to pay the taxes necessary to cover the expense of government and have refused to elect representatives who would balance the budget.

Now that you are retired, you want more money from the government, but do not want to pay down the debt accumulated when you were younger. Money has seduced your generation to the point that it has steered you away from the financial wisdom your parents and grandparents knew. In addition, you have done nothing for the younger generation to help them cover the expense of your retirement, the expense of paying down the debt, and the expense of running the government. The bottom line is that you have voted yourself benefits at the expense of younger generations and the future of the country.

In addition, a prevailing position that you, the older generation, have adopted is, "I'm not going to worry about it because I only have a few more years to live anyway." This attitude is a disservice to not only the generations that will follow, but it also damages and undercuts the entire democratic philosophy that has been advancing throughout humankind's attempt to elevate itself. Change is necessary in the Constitution to protect future generations from this ruinous, poisonous attitude.

On another topic, during the late 1970s, your generation experienced firsthand the consequences of this country's reliance on foreign oil. Yet you have done almost nothing in the way of energy conservation to move this country away from its weakness of being dependent on foreign oil. You must realize that no matter how low the price

of oil goes, imported oil increases the trade deficit, thus
decreasing the money supply within the economy and
pushing the government to borrow or print more money to
keep your standard of living artificially high.

　　　More so than anyone else, it is YOU—your
willingness to change your way of thinking, your willingness
to give back and sacrifice, your willingness to make good on
the debt and reduce dependency on foreign oil through
conservation—who can save this country from the evil
effects of debt and trade deficits. Action by YOU, more than
any other generation, can reduce the future financial suffering
of your children, grandchildren, and great-grandchildren.
Without your generation's willingness to change, your
progeny will lose their freedom and their country. And that
will be your legacy—leaving the next generations with slave-
instituting, freedom-robbing, life-deteriorating debt.

Grievances against the News Media

You in the news media have failed your country. You have given the two financially incompetent political parties all the attention, thus strongly suggesting to the citizens that these are the only parties they should vote for. You have ignored smaller political parties that have endorsed financial responsibility as one of their platforms; these political parties are thrown aside by you as unimportant.

You have recognized the wrongness of the two parties' financial actions as incidents rather than a larger pattern of total financial neglect. You have labeled the political parties "left" and "right" while ignoring the more important labels of "fiscally responsible" and "fiscally irresponsible" (only the "fiscally irresponsible" has power in Washington at this time.)

In addition, some of your cohorts expound the fallacy to the citizens that "debt doesn't matter," that "we just owe it to ourselves." You who know better have let this deception spread without aggressive rebuttal. As a result, a relatively large number of citizens believe this. Permit the following attempt to throw some water of reason on this wicked witch of the west notion.

It should be kept in mind that if it is true—that the US debt does not matter—then it is reasonable to say debt has no limit and can keep growing infinitely. Therefore, if this works for the United States today, there is no reason why it would not work positively for any country in the world. (Present-day Greece comes to mind.) Logically, if this works in the present day, then it must have been available to work in past millennia also.

However, there is no recorded history of a nation or empire having existed for any lengthy amount of time with

1   the policy of building debt. Have we, with thousands of years
2   of human experience behind us, just discovered for ourselves
3   that debt can go to infinity? Were men of earlier centuries just
4   too ignorant to figure out that they could have gone into
5   huge debt, saving their countrymen a lot of suffering and
6   grief? No.

7   In about 300 BC, Euclid, an ancient Greek scholar
8   working in Alexandria, proved that there were an infinite
9   number of prime numbers (numbers that are divisible only by
10   one and itself).[17] This was extraordinary thinking. That was
11   over 2,000 years ago. Since that time, men have built up and
12   toppled empires and civilizations. Courageous men
13   discovered and mapped out a new hemisphere. All kinds of
14   men and women thought of great inventions and made great
15   discoveries. Brilliant military officers invented new ways of
16   fighting wars. Scientists and mathematicians expanded
17   mankind's knowledge about medicine, space, engineering,
18   psychology, meteorology, etc., and have been doing so for a
19   very long time. Yet among these remarkable achievements,
20   from the time of Euclid to the present, no one has proved
21   that debt can go to infinity. And those who tried to prove this
22   in actual practice met with ruinous consequences. The
23   Founding Fathers of this nation often pointed out that high
24   debt led to dilapidating situations for the countries of
25   Europe.

26   You of the news media can now hopefully see the
27   fabricated financial doctrine of "we just owe it to ourselves"
28   for what it is—very poisonous opium for the people.

29   Your industry has the smartest communicators in the

---

[17] Singh, Simon, *The Simpsons and Their Mathematical Secrets*, Bloomsbury: New York, 2013, p. 11.

country. Yet you seem to have no inkling that the national debt can destroy the freedom of the people—including the freedom of the press.

Re-evaluating and changing your philosophy concerning how your industry presents politicians and political parties could be a very good thing for the people and the future of this nation.

Grievances against Citizens who support Illegal Immigration

It was the trade surpluses during the first 200 years of this country's existence that allowed immigrants to be integrated into our economy with positive results. With little hesitation, this country was able to absorb these great surges of humanity. No longer.

You must realize that our country has not had a trade surplus for over 30 years. The country's current ability to handle the recent influx of illegal immigrants is a false perception caused by the astronomical borrowing of money by the central government. The Republicans and Democrats in Congress borrow in order to offset the loss of money and jobs from our economy through the imprudent trade agreements they have made.

Your ideas about helping immigrants are virtuous, but your support of illegal immigration is counterproductive to the humaneness you are trying to project. You must realize that we have the appearance of being a rich country, but we are not. Rich countries do not have astronomical debt or precipitous trade deficits.

When our economy finally adjusts to the negative finances of the government, a huge humanitarian disaster will take place. The illegal immigrants will bear the greatest suffering.

You must realize that what seems humane today will cause a greater humanitarian backlash later; it is an eventuality in the making. It will overwhelmingly subvert your current humanitarian efforts. Due to this very predictable future, it is more humane to stop people from illegally immigrating into the country. And that is what you should do—help stop illegal immigration. Also, you should focus on helping legal

immigrants begin to plan and prepare for the great
humanitarian disaster that is waiting to befall the citizens and
the country once the economy readjusts to financial reality.

Grievances against Citizens who want a Higher Minimum Wage

You do not seem to understand that a higher minimum wage in the United States will not change the minimum wages in China, India, South Korea, Brazil, Italy, etc. You have failed to realize that foreign countries have not only been competing for this country's manufacturing jobs, but have been winning this competition. The main reason for this is that their workers receive lower wages—they have outbid us on jobs.

You (as well as prominent economists) have failed to recognize that when the minimum wage goes up and manufacturing jobs leave the country, Congress borrows more money to throw into the economy to offset this loss. The borrowed money creates jobs that do not lead to trade surpluses; therefore, they cannot be sustained by the marketplace. Thus, it falsely appears that raising the minimum wage has no negative effect on the job market or the economy, when in fact it is helping to destroy the financial base of the country by adding to the debt. A trade deficit is an indicator of the loss of jobs. When there is a trade deficit, the minimum wage should be decreased, not increased. It should continue to be decreased until the point where there is a trade surplus for the nation.

You must understand that it is trade surpluses that create and maintain rich countries. You need to support elected representatives who will fight for trade surpluses. Only when there are trade surpluses should there be an increase of the minimum wage. Otherwise, increasing the minimum wage when there are trade deficits undermines the entire nation's economy and undermines future liberty.

On yet another level, your goal to help low-wage

earners earn more is commendable, but your strategy is erroneous. Your focus should be on increasing the education and skills of low-paid workers. Your focus should be on emphasizing the importance of the first 12 years of public education and its ties to determining future earnings. You should be focused on changing the education system if it does not yield the real-world results of getting citizens ready for higher-paid work and higher forms of education. The ironic fact that politicians are seeking low-paid, high-skilled foreign workers to enter the country's workforce while millions of citizens are on food stamps and are unemployed or underemployed, is a strong indicator that our educational system has failed to support our nation's businesses, and with that, our future liberties.

This is what you should be focused on—better ways of increasing the skills and education of our citizens—instead of focusing on the superficial action of increasing the minimum wage.

Grievances against Citizens who support and run the Military-Industrial Complex

You have been seduced by money and you appear to care only for profit. You have no fear of wars, and commercialize war by creating and combating imaginary monsters like Iraq. You encourage the harassment and antagonization of the governments of foreign countries, and interpret different countries' actions in the worst possible light, setting the stage for unjust and illogical escalations of hostilities—similar to pre-World War I events.[18] This makes our own land, from sea to sea, the potential for a theater for a major war.

You then use these as justifications to increase military spending, thereby creating profit for yourself.

All the while, you have helped to create the true monster—debt—and are allowing it to consume the nation's wealth and well-being.

Also, you have helped orchestrate the elimination of two checks and balances of military action. First, by influencing representatives of the two political parties, you have helped to eliminate the military draft, replacing it with a well-paid, professional, all-voluntary force. (Which, by the way, citizens cannot afford and don't want to pay for.) Secondly, you have indefinitely postponed the increase in taxes needed to cover military costs. This avoids military action from undergoing the solid checks and balances of serious public scrutiny—checks and balances that should never have been devitalized and that the Founding Fathers, as

---

[18] Allison, Graham and Simes, Dimitri K. "Stumbling to War," *The National Interest*, magazine, Number 137, May/June 2015: pp. 9-21, The Center for the National Interest.

well as past presidents and generals (like Dwight Eisenhower
and George Washington) would insist be in place. Without
these checks and balances, ordinary citizens will continue to
be disconnected from the consequences of military decisions.
The citizens will then accept war with little anxiety, which in
turn paves the way for you and your representatives to raid
the United States Treasury under the pretense of protecting
the country. It paves the way for those in power to create
conflicts that do not help humanity in any way, shape, or
form.

One of your arguments for spending borrowed
money on the military over the last 35 years has been job
creation. However, with some scrutiny, you would see that
those jobs have not led to a trade surplus as they did after
World War II. These types of jobs make the country much
weaker because they are created with money from taxpayers
and future generations rather than from surpluses gained
from international trade and the marketplace. Therefore, this
economic argument for military spending is unsound.

You have good reason to receive federal financing,
primarily to protect this nation; however, your goal of having
a strong military by borrowing exorbitant sums of money
runs counter to protecting the future of this nation and the
US Constitution. Stop. Think. The contradiction is there in
front of you. You who are most fervent for a strong military
and who advocate military action around the globe are also
ardently against raising taxes to pay for these expenses, thus
undermining the security and stability of this nation that the
military is supposed to defend! The spending of huge sums of
borrowed money that the public may not have the will or
ability to pay back absolutely undermines your mission to
protect this country. The debt will eventually destabilize the

United States government.

You must understand that the foremost enemy of this nation is self-sabotaging debt. No nation or group of people comes near to posing the kind of threat that debt does; it can vaporize the economy—and with that, topple our government. It is your duty to fight this enemy of the United States and the US Constitution.

The nation can no longer endure this dereliction of financial duty.

You need to recognize that your seduction by money has put the health of the Union of Fifty States at risk. You must begin to realize the limits of government finance, and what the citizens are able and willing to pay for. You must begin to support political representatives who will abide by financial limits. You must do everything you can to reduce all military costs.

Understand, it is the wise government that endeavors to acquire financial surpluses and build good credit ratings with its people and foreign sources. This allows reserved energies (as well as the accumulation of psychological vitalities of the citizens) to build up, so in the event that military power MUST be used, it can be focused at the right time, at the right place, to win large, meaningful, and just wars. Small or meaningless conflicts can drain these reserve energies. Without prior years of government financial prudence, the military cannot be sustained for very long in the field of battle against a formidable enemy. This is when sustainability will be needed the most. Therefore, in the country's current financial position, it would be prudent to eschew building hostilities against other countries—especially against large nations.

Those citizens who are members of the military, who

1 have seen the sacrifice and trauma to their fellow warriors
2 and friends, and who are apprehensive and cautious about
3 military actions and wars, need to become leaders in the
4 civilian world and fight against those who choose war for
5 profit. Otherwise, the result of doing nothing will likely
6 nullify all the sacrifices of all generations of veterans, past and
7 present.

Grievances against Citizens who say, "You have been telling us for years about an economic and political meltdown. Unless you tell us when it will occur, it will not occur."

The habits of overeating, abusing alcohol, and smoking can eventually lead to medical complications in the future of a human life. Evidence shows these habits will increase the likelihood of diseases. Suffering that could have been prevented will occur sometime in the future if these habits are not changed. But the ultimate punishment for continuing these habits is a shortened life. The deleterious health effects of these habits do not show up the next day or the next year, but decades later. There is no pinpointing when—what day or year you will get diagnosed with heart disease, kidney disease, or lung cancer. However, this does not mean a preemptive strike on these unhealthy habits should not be addressed today.

Just like these health concerns, certain habits in an economy and a democratic society can lead to the end of their life cycle; that is, to the end of freedom and self-rule. And just like health problems, it cannot be pinpointed when the life of an economy or democracy will end. However, we do know what habits are damaging to the future of economies and democracies—the habit of the government overspending without considering acquiring surpluses; the habit of democratic rulers lying to and misleading citizens; the habit of manipulating or violating principles of freedom by the rulers; and the habit of citizens depending on government instead of government depending on citizens, are but a few of these deadly habits.

It is human nature to avoid worry and anxiety, especially when change is needed. Personal change and

change within our workplace can be very stressful—after all, change can be unpredictable, and we are dealing with unknowns.

However, worrying can be a beneficial thing if we substitute the anxiety with actions that will deter future problems from happening. This takes bravery. Worrying is harmful if it leads to excuses and activities that leave the future threat untouched and cause us to forget them. Forgetting harmful health habits does not solve the health problems; forgetting harmful government habits does not solve governmental problems.

In our economy and democracy, there is a responsibility on citizens to act; it is within our grasp and it is our duty to change things that are not right. The German people chose not to worry about what the Nazi government was doing. We Americans must not make that same choice. In this economy and democracy, it is the citizen's responsibility to gain understanding and acquire the will and the courage to change.

The Declaration of Independence warns us of the inclination of humans to not want to change their government. The redundancy of repeating this fact in this book underscores the very importance of the awareness and acknowledgment of this inclination in human nature. This inclination leads to a glut of excuses and a scarcity of action. However, we have the human intelligence to overcome our destructive inclinations. Many of us have been through drastic changes in our lives and have survived. For our country, future change will be utterly traumatic, but we can and will survive.

1   In evaluating patriotism, here is a question when

2 considering transforming the nation; are we really "the home

3 of the brave" or is that song out of date?

❧

The Last Grievance—against Citizens

$\mathcal{I}$n our human function within our society—as teachers, clergy, accountants, soldiers, voters, politicians, business leaders, etc.—the comfort, contentment, and confidence that money offers have seduced, hypnotized, and bribed these elements of ourselves into ignoring the inappropriateness of Congress' spending habits and their creation of harmful trade agreements. Every corner and function within our society has been overrun by the tainted money Congress distributes. The money makes our heads swell; we think confidently about ourselves. We consider people of other countries as inferior, and we ignore the abysmal financial situation the two financially inept national parties have put our country in.

Our leaders have advertised and promoted the notion that we are an exceptional country and people. However, there is no doubt that we, as a people, have traded our humility for hubris, foresight for thoughtlessness, and our moral spirit for worldly objects. We have forgotten our country and, in doing so, failed our country. We, as a modern people, have been sustaining the thought of "what can the country can do for me?" rather than what President Kennedy promoted, which was what you can do for your country. Our modern thinking is not the characteristic of an exceptional country at all. What our current mind-set is, is a major setback for self-rule.

Can we become an exceptional people? Are we willing to take responsibility for our country's debt, unlike so many other nations throughout history? Are we willing to give up the artificially high standard of living that has been propped

up by the borrowing and printing of money? Will we make it a priority to learn from the patterns of self-destructive human behavior that have existed since antiquity and take advantage of these insights?

Perhaps we will prove that we are not exceptional at all, and instead behave like any other country or empire from world history. We will sit back and allow our human inclinations and flaws to dictate our fate without making any effort to change, then turn and blame others for our economic and political predicament. Do we truly live in a forgotten country—forgotten by the majority of citizens?

If the United States and its citizens are indeed exceptional, as our politicians proclaim, this label expresses that we should stand humbly but firmly upright and make the hard decision of biting the financial bullet. This means transforming our forgotten country. We should not act like the people of present-day Greece and deny our financial responsibility. We must place upon ourselves the responsibility of implementing austerity in order to make up for our past decisions of consenting to the indebtedness our representatives have put us in. It is the moral and just thing to do; it is our obligation.

To do this, we need to begin to support and campaign for financial checks and balances to be added to the Constitution. The grounds for doing an end-round around Congress to accomplish this have been stated. Injecting financial temperance into the political system at the Constitutional level will no doubt be an arduous undertaking, but for the sake of the country, for the sake of our children and their children, for the preservation of the Union, for the protection of liberty and democracy—this is what we must do.

Part 4.
Changing a Fate Predicted:
Forging a New Destiny

$\mathcal{T}$he nation's forefathers did what they could to build the framework of a solid government for future generations by writing the Constitution. We are in possession of what they accomplished. But the national Republican and Democratic parties of this day have exposed severe flaws in the Constitution. By putting the country into debt amounting to more than 18 trillion dollars, and by accumulating a negative trade balance of more than 9 trillion dollars (Exhibit A and B at the front of the book), the two parties are continuing the process of undermining domestic tranquility, destroying the common defense, demoting the general welfare, and securing the curse of servitude for our posterity and ourselves. The Democratic and Republican parties have, no doubt, been committing high crimes and misdemeanors against the Union of Fifty States for a long time—no one has been stopping them.

The Constitution does explicitly gives Congress full power of ownership over the nation's credit card, but the founders did not mean for Congress to spend without limit. The founders relied on the financial conscience and wisdom of the representatives to keep us out of perpetual debt, which many nations prior to the birth of ours had succumbed to. It is uncharacteristic of the Founding Fathers to place no concrete check or balance within the Constitution concerning a subject of this nature—but that is what they have done. They added no articles to the Constitution that would prevent Congress (or a mass of individual citizens) from abandoning financial responsibly.

And so, unlike previous generations of representatives, the members of Congress of the last 35 years have been unable to maintain financial judiciousness and

integrity. Financial conscience has withered away. This is something the Founding Fathers left for us to deal with, but we citizens have done nothing thus far. We must begin to seriously implement one of the principles our country was founded on—that is, the principle of separation of power. In particular, the separation of financial power.

Though the men and women in the two national parties hold the keys to unlocking the Constitution for change, it is clear that Congress will never call for a Constitutional Convention, for they and their supporting lobbyists and constituencies currently prosper from irresponsible deficit spending—morality and wisdom are absent.

Also, with Congress being seemingly unaware of the severe consequences of financial irresponsibility—the forfeiting of peace and stability—changing the Constitution is one of the furthest things from their minds.

Unlike the exceptional mind-set of George Washington, our legislators' instincts will lead them to become relentless in defending their own power, which means the continuation of spending of borrowed money and the printing of more currency to bribe the public.

Clearly, power is as addictive as any drug. The spending power that Congress has abused for so long needs to be swiftly removed. We should endeavor to transform the current Congressional culture into a fiscally conscientious culture. We should wish and pray to accomplish this through peaceful constitutional change and not through other forms of calamitous actions. A quote from Anti-Federalist No. 46 (by An Old WHIG) encourages us to avoid a breakdown in civility:

"...It appears that no other power on earth can dictate to them, or control them, unless by force; and force, either internal or external, is one of those calamities which every good man would wish his country at all times to be delivered from."

Let this be a notification to citizens of this nation: considering that the current political powers have been abusing their financial authority for decades, through either stratagem or ignorance, you, the good people of this nation, are fully authorized to change the Constitution. Let there be no hesitation in thought on this matter. Dissolving the comfort of our relationship and allegiance to the two major national political parties will most likely be required.

Hence, to change the Constitution, a new assembly of sagacious and virtuous men from the states needs to be selected and organized. They will have to consider very basic questions: What exactly is government? What is the ideal government? What did the original Founding Fathers know of this topic?[19] What does it mean to be a citizen? What should be expected of citizens in our society? These basic questions and more will have to be thought through by our New Age Founding Fathers.

But first, in order to create this assembly of the wisest men from the states, one of the fifty states has to take a leadership role. This single state in the Union has to have citizens of great courage, fortitude, and energy in order to

---

[19] A list of publications that influenced the Founding Fathers can be seen at: http://www.thefederalistpapers.org/founding-father-influences

1 stand firm against the two main political parties in
2 Washington, DC, and their bureaucracy. Declarations of
3 support and commitment must come quickly from other
4 states.

5   If no transformation takes place, this union of states
6 will end like a Shakespearean tragedy—ugly and venomous.
7 The consequences of the continued abuse of financial power
8 by the two national political parties will lead to the drying out
9 of the branches of the tree of liberty, and can cause stars to
10 fall off the nation's flag. These consequences are no longer in
11 the distant future.

12   And that is why, fellow citizens, we must put forth
13 prodigious amounts of courage and energy into changing the
14 Constitution. We must be proactive and not wait for the
15 man-made economic disaster to occur naturally before
16 beginning to take action. The grounds for why
17 transformation must take place have been laid out—they are
18 sturdy.

19   Change is afoot, but do not despair. Let there be no
20 doubt that we can change. It will take the power of families,
21 friends, neighbors, and community fellowship to recover and
22 reinvent the operations of the government and our society;
23 intentional change must come from the grassroots. We will
24 have to become closer to the people we know. We will need
25 to rely on the help of each other rather than the national
26 government.

27   Our whole society can enact positive change and
28 advance human existence by adopting new philosophies,
29 recommitting to old principles, and resurrecting a religious
30 morality towards fiduciary matters. We must show the rest of
31 humanity that in our democracy, in our republic, we can be
32 responsible for remedying our own turmoil, and that we can

1   govern ourselves with financial responsibility. We must show
2   the rest of the world that ruinous past decisions can
3   eventually result in positive effects on society and its citizens,
4   and the world. We can become a stronger nation by enduring
5   and triumphing over the coming adversity together.
6   With prayers to the heavens, we can and will institute
7   a more perfect Union for the 50 states—and for mankind.

QUOTES AND COMMENTS

$\mathcal{F}$or the voting citizens in our democracy, knowing the founding principles on which our government system is based is more important than knowing what is in the Constitution. The principles give us the rules and guidelines we need to protect our freedom and liberty from our own ruinous human instincts and inclinations.[20] This kind of study has been severely lacking within our great educational institutions.

Coaches of sports teams carry a set of what they personally believe are winning principles to their team—and these principles are imposed upon their team. If their team falls off the path by failing to follow these principles, the coach is there to steer the team back on the path through the use of attitude adjustment activities and warnings. For example, if a team becomes content and complacent because they think they are great, the coach may impose extra practice time, as well as inundate the team with verbal assaults, in the hope of steering them back on the proper path of working hard and not taking anything for granted. If the coach does not move to correct the team, a lonely and not particularly well-performing team could suddenly upset them in a defining game, changing their desired destiny.

Voting citizens of democracies do not have a coach to guide them. Therefore, citizens of democracies—of all democracies—need to know the principles of maintaining a democracy. It is this knowledge of founding principles that can keep a democratic people on the path to freedom and liberty, and will stop the cycle of human behaviors that have

---

[20] The book, *The 5,000-Year Leap* offers 28 principles.

led to failed democracies throughout human history. Failing
to follow these principles will slowly and steadily lead to the
freedoms being dissolved.[21]

Important sayings and quotes can remind us of these
principles and provide warnings on what will transpire if the
principles are not upheld.

Note that without strong knowledge of democratic
principles by voting citizens, those in power can slowly
change and manipulate principles to their personal advantage
without the citizens questioning the change.[22] Voting citizens
armed with principles will have the ability to know if elected
representatives maintain the principles and philosophies that
reflect the wisdom of these passages and the like, and vote to
reverse trends that lead to the slow abandonment of
principles.

A mandatory Constitutional Convention every 20
years can help ensure that principles do not get manipulated
by the people that rule. The New Age Founding Fathers will
indeed need to know the founding principles of freedom to
be able to adjust the Constitution wisely.

Our educational institutions should begin to require
the following passages, as well as many other quotes and
passages based on principles of freedom, be included
permanently in their curricula. These quotes and similar text
should be taught from the lowest, right up to and especially at
the highest levels of education, where many of our country's
leaders get their advanced education. These passages should
remind us that our democracy, liberty, and freedom are fragile

---

[21] *The Anti-Federalist Papers* and *The Federalist Papers* provide real-world examples of the implementation and absence of specific principles from past governments.
[22] The book *Animal Farm* brings attention to this flaw in human society.

and are subject to human whims, moods, and temperaments. So much of freedom depends upon the psychological state of whole generations that the teaching of these principles must be widespread and intense.

Here are some important quotes to be considered relating to the principles of freedom and liberty. The first few have comments.

> *The American Republic will endure until the day Congress discovers that it can bribe the public with the public's money.*[23]
> —Alexis de Tocqueville

∽

COMMENT: This quote accurately predicted the actions of today's two national parties. Those citizens who have been alert would mark the early 1980s as when the bribery came into full swing—when debt became a chronic feature of this nation. It is when the majority of the citizenry began voting based on what they received from Congress rather than on what was good for the country. The two parties continue the flow of bribery money into public pockets. The problem with this "easy money," as the quote predicts, is that it is detrimental to the continued existence of this republic.

---

[23] Good Reads, Democracy in America Quotes, 2015.
http://www.goodreads.com/author/quotes/465.Alexis_de_Tocqueville (A confirming source of the quote was not located.)

> *It [the power of government] covers the surface of society with a network of small complicated rules, minute and uniform, through which the most original minds and the most energetic characters cannot penetrate... ...It does not tyrannize but it compresses, enervates, extinguishes, and stupefies a people, till each nation is reduced to nothing better than a flock of timid and industrious animals, of which the government is the shepherd.[24]*
>
> —Alexis de Tocqueville

∽

COMMENT: The thousands of pages of the Affordable Care Act, the thousands of pages of the nation's tax code, and the tens of thousands of pages that are absolutely necessary to explain and clarify each of these are real-world examples of exactly what the quote says. This is why the quotes from Tocqueville and other authors should be studied by all citizens—they allow the chance for wisdom to be applied to decisions having to do with the governing of our country, and allow citizens to recognize when wisdom is not applied.

Of course, this situation described in the quote does not bode well for the future of freedom and liberty. (Will our elected officials and the bureaucrats working for us in Washington, DC, be willing to give up the kind of power these documents give them? ...Not without a fight.)

---

[24] Tocqueville, Alex de. *Democracy In America, Volume 2*, The Project Gutenberg, E-book #816, 2006, Henry Reeve, translator. p. 319, Vol 2.

> *In the United States I am not sure that the people would choose men of superior abilities even if they wished to be elected; but it is certain that candidates of this description do not come forward.* [25]
> —Alexis de Tocqueville, Democracy in America

COMMENT: The best citizens to lead this nation are hidden. It is up to us, the common citizens, to seek them out and convince them they must enter into political life. It is up to us to find the best people, and not just leave it up to the two political parties to force candidates on us, leaving us to choose the lesser of two evils rather than the best this country has to offer. We must examine and change our philosophy towards the two-party system because it just is not working. It is time to look outside the comfort of the two-party system with the approach that it is for the betterment of the country.

The best people for the country are overlooked by the general population "for a variety of biased reasons and perceived flaws"[26]—appearance, personality, material

[25] Tocqueville, de Alexis. *Democracy in America*. American Studies at the University of Virginia. Chapter 13-Government of the Democracy in America, section-Public Officers under the Control of the American Democracy. Creation of machine-readable version: Electronic edition deposited and marked-up by ASGRP, the American Studies Programs at the University of Virginia, June 1, 1997. From the Henry Reeve Translation, revised and corrected, 1899. http://xroads.virginia.edu/~HYPER/DETOC/1_ch13.htm
[26] *Moneyball*, directed by Bennett Miller, screenplay by Steven Zaillian and Aaron Sorkin, based on the book *Moneyball* by Michael Lewis, featuring Brad (Footnote continued on next page...)

holdings, ideologies, etc. These may not have anything to do with how well the individuals would lead this country.

Two examples of ideologies that skew our perception of candidates are abortion and gun control. Strictly voting for candidates that are for or against these ideologies will not put the best leaders in Washington, DC. We, as citizens, sometimes have to vote against our ideologies. We need instead to look for candidates that have such virtues as frugality, humility, and perhaps most important for a democracy, integrity. Candidates should also discern and apply justice, and have resolve as well as other virtues.

Can we, as individuals, put on the sidelines our ideologies while determining who is the best person to lead this country? There will be great difficulty in finding men and women who have the Founding Fathers' superior characteristics of wisdom, foresight, integrity, and knowledge, in addition to not having been "touched" by the tainted money of Congress. But that is exactly what we must do in order to initiate the proper changes to our bankrupt country.

Pitt and Jonah Hill. Columbia Pictures, produced by Michael De Luca, Rachael Horovitz, and Brad Pitt, 2011.

> *Everybody feels the evil, but no one has courage or energy enough to seek the cure.*[27]
> —Alexis de Tocqueville, Democracy in America

COMMENT: Most citizens feel this way, right? We know the national debt is evil. We know we should be purchasing "Made in USA" products so as to make the economy stronger without the government having to borrow money. We know Congress has made horrendously bad trade agreements and wastes money beyond comprehension. We know the two parties are setting us up for an uncontrollable downfall.

But do we even want the cure? Would we rather wait in the comfort of our familiarity with daily life and just let nature take its course? The Declaration of Independence says that is what man has the tendency to do. After all, the cure will mean moving into unfamiliar territory, and without question, it will hurt—so much so, it will feel as if it is worse than the disease. In many cases, the cure will eliminate our current livelihoods; it will force us to find or make new jobs for ourselves; it will lower our standard of living; it will eliminate many benefits that the government currently hands out; it will destroy our comfort and break our hearts. But that will also happen if we do nothing.

The cure is not worse, and will never be worse than

---

[27] Tocqueville, Alexis, *Democracy In America, Volume 1*, The Project Gutenberg, EBook, Translator: Henry **Reeve**. p. 11, Vol 1. Release Date: January 21, 2006 [EBook #815] Last updated: February 12, 2012.

1   this disease. By moving to cure the financial problems, we
2   retain freedom of speech and expression, freedom of the
3   press and assembly, and freedom of religion and petition. We
4   retain a say in our government. We will still have hope for
5   rebuilding a new and better future for our descendants. We
6   will feel some sense of control, as small as it may be. We can
7   retain our human spirit knowing the whole of mankind will
8   be better off if we can maintain the Union of Fifty States and
9   get through the coming turmoil.
10   We lose most of this if we wait for nature to take its
11   course.

About the Anti-Federalist Papers

It is *The Anti-Federalist Papers* that brings forth the weaknesses of this federated union of states. It is *The Federalist Papers* that brings to the forefront mostly strengths of the Constitution. *The Anti-Federalist Papers* get less notoriety than *The Federalist Papers*, however, it should be studied just as much. Just like any sports team knows, knowing your weaknesses is just as important as knowing your strengths. Knowing both strengths and weaknesses of having freedom and living in a republic lays a foundation for continued long-term success.

One theme that runs through *The Anti-Federalist Papers* is the concern for how easily man gets corrupted by power. We all know money is power. The trillions of dollars of debt have corrupted many of us in ways that are hard for us to see within ourselves. How do we become aware and acknowledge the corruption within ourselves? Unfortunately, it is well concealed and protected in our own reasons and aims. All of the people of this country who are receiving any money or benefits (such as paychecks, pensions, loans, food stamps, etc.) from our bankrupted government should deeply evaluate the question of their own personal level of corruption.

For your consideration, here are quotes from *The Anti-Federalist Papers.*[28]

---

[28]These quotes can also be found on *Federalist vs. Anti-Federalist Study Guide* https://www.monticellocollege.org/sites/default/files/files/federalist-vs-anti-federalist.pdf

Is human nature above self-interest?

A GEORGIAN

Anti-Federalist #54

∽∾

Men may always be too cautious to commit alarming and glaring iniquities; but they, as well as systems, are liable to be corrupted by slow degrees.

THE FEDERAL FARMER

Anti-Federalist #56

∽∾

For power is a very intoxicating thing, and has made many a man do unwarrantable actions, which before he was invested with it, he had no thoughts of doing.

AMICUS

Anti-Federalist #53

∽∾

...For the great body of the people never steadily attend to the operations of government....

CENTINEL

Anti-Federalist #47

∽∾

> *A government possessed of more power than its constituent parts justify, will not only probably abuse it, but be unequal to bear its own burden; it may as soon be destroyed by the pressure of power, as languish and perish for want of it.*

THE FEDERAL FARMER, by Richard Henry Lee
Anti-Federalist #41-43

> *May heaven inspire you with wisdom, union, moderation and firmness, and give you hearts to make a proper estimate of your invaluable privileges, and preserve them to you, to be transmitted to your posterity unimpaired, and may they be maintained in this our country, while the Sun and Moon endure.*

A PLEBEIAN by Melancthon Smith
Anti-Federalist #85

> *I wish for nothing more than a good government and a constitution under which our liberties will be perfectly safe.*

AMICUS
Anti-Federalist #53

FINAL THOUGHTS

The two parties have built an "iron castle of corruption"—a formidable fortress of financial infidelity. And to protect their raiding of the U.S. Treasury, a moat of entangled bureaucracy has been constructed; walls of deceit have been built to hide what financial corruptible acts are going on inside. Archers are hired to sling political arrows at anyone or any organization who attempts to break through the walls. A castle door is built to let in lobbyists and anyone with enough money; and black knights are financially trained to distribute gifts of tainted money to the common citizens so they will not start an uprising. All the while, the two parties are raiding the treasury under the veil of American Nationalism.

James S. Sitnik

For The Vigilant Citizen

1 *T*ake notes.
2 Study ideas.
3 Write your thoughts and explanations.
4 Read philosophies and texts on governments.
5 Write and note significant dialogs.
6 Contemplate…
7 Formulate solutions in writing.
8 *T*hen...
9

James S. Sitnik

∽§

Bibliography

Abramoff, Jack. *Jack Abramoff: The Lobbyist's Playbook Or How to Buy Your Own Congressperson, 60 Minutes*, CBS Correspondent Lesley Stahl, producer Ira Rose. Nov. 6, 2011. Television.

Allyson Ambrose. *5 Steps to 5 - 500 AP English Language Questions* , The McGraw-Hill Companies, Inc., 2011.
Passage 1c: Benjamin Franklin, The Autobiography of Benjamin Franklin
Passage 2b: Thomas Carlyle, On Heroes, Hero-Worship and the Heroic in History
Passage 2c: Winston Churchill, The Approaching Conflict
Passage 2d: Thomas Babington Macaulay, Hallam's History
Passage 3a: Matthew Arnold, The Function of Criticism at the Current Time
Passage 3b: Ralph Waldo Emerson, Shakespeare; or, the Poet
Passage 3d: Walter Pater, Studies in the History of the Renaissance
Passage 3e: John Ruskin, Of the Pathetic Fallacy
Passage 4b: Francis Bacon, Of Marriage and Single Life
Passage 4d: Charles Lamb, The Two Races of Men
Passage 4e: Michel de Montaigne, Of the Punishment of Cowardice
Passage 6a: Thomas Jefferson, Sixth State of the Union Address
Passage 6b: John Stuart Mill, Considerations on Representative Government
Passage 6c: Thomas Paine, Common Sense
Passage 6d: Alexis de Tocqueville, Democracy in America, Volume 1
Passage 7a: Niccolo Machiavelli, The Prince
Passage 7b: Thomas More, Utopia
Passage 7c: Thomas Hobbes, Leviathan
Passage 7d: John Milton, Areopagitica
Passage 8a: Edward Gibbon, The History of the Decline and Fall of the Roman Empire
Passage 8c: John Locke, Second Treatise on Government
Passage 9b: John Henry Newman, Private Judgement
Passage 9d: Henry David Thoreau, Civil Disobedience
Passage 10d: George Santayana, The Life of Reason

Bacevich, Andrew J. *The Limits of Power, The End of American Exceptionalism*, Metropolitan Books, Henry Holt and Company, New York, 2008.

Bellamy, Richard. *Citizenship - A Very Short Introduction*, Oxford University

Press, Oxford, UK, 2008. 1-99.

Brands, H. W. *Benjamin Franklin – The Original American*, Barnes & Noble Publishing, United States, 2004, audio CD.

Buchanan, Patrick J. *A Republic, Not an Empire – Reclaiming America's Destiny*, Regnery Publishing, Inc., Washington, DC, 1999.

Canterbery, E. Ray. *A Brief History of Economics: Artful Approaches to the Dismal Science*, World Scientific. New Jersey, 2001.

Cook, William R. *Machiavelli in Context*, The Teaching Company. audio CD. 2006.

Duhigg, Charles. *The Power of Habit – Why We Do What We Do In Life and Business*, Random House, New York, 2012.

Dweck, Carol S. *Mindset, The New Psychology of Success.* Ballantine Books, New York, 2006.

Elowitz, Larry. *Introduction to Government*, HarperCollins Publishers, Inc., New York, 1992.

Fears, J. Rufus. *The Wisdom of History*, The Teaching Company, audio CDs 1 and 2. 2007.

Fromm, Erick. *Escape From Freedom.* Henry Holt and Company, New York, 1969.

Founding Fathers, The. *The Anti-Federalist Papers*, ReadaClassic.com, Layout and cover copyright 2010.

Hamilton, James, Madison, James, and John Jay. *The Federalist Papers.*

Project Gutenberg, www.gutenberg.net, Ebook #18, 1991. pp 1-102.

Harl, Kenneth W. *The Peloponnesian War*, The Teaching Company, DVD, 2007.

Heilbrunn, Jacob. *The National Interest*, Number 128, Nov/Dec 2013, The Center for the National Interest, Washington, DC. 2013.

Heilbrunn, Jacob. *The National Interest*, Number 131, May/June 2014, The Center for the National Interest, Washington, DC, 2014.

Heilbrunn, Jacob. *The National Interest*, Number 135, Jan/Feb 2015, The Center for the National Interest, Washington, DC, 2015.

Ignatius, Adi. *Harvard Business Review - OnPoint - Leading Change – What Works & What Doesn't*, Harvard Business School Publishing

Corporation, Boston. Winter 2014 issue, 2014.

Inside Job. Dir. Charles Ferguson, SONY Pictures Classics, 2010, DVD Film

Koterski, Joseph. *The Ethics of Aristotle,* The Teaching Company, audio CD. 2001.

Kaplan, Joshua. *Codes of Power – Political Thought from Plato's Cave to Game Theory,* Barnes & Noble Publishing, United States, 2006, audio CD.

Lincoln, Abraham. *Abraham Lincoln, The Gettysburg Address and other Writings,* Fall River Press, New York, 2013.

Lipsky, Seth. *The Citizen's Constitution, An Annotated Guide,* Basic Books, New York, 2009.

McElvaine, Robert S. *The Great Depression, America, 1929-1941,* Time Books, New York, 1983.

Martin, Randy, Producer; Cannon, Mark, Director. *Engineering an Empire – The Complete Series,* Host: Peter Weller, DVD.

Muller, Jerry Z. *Thinking About Capitalism,* The Teaching Company, Chantilly, Virginia, 2008. Audio CD.

Monk, Linda R. *The Words We Live By – Your Annotated Guide to the Constitution,* Hyperion, New York, 2003.

Michael MacDonald and Christopher Whitestone, *The Silver Bomb, The End of Paper Wealth is Upon Us,* An independently published book, 2012.

Merry, Robert W. *The National Interest,* Number 124, Mar/Apr 2013, The Center for the National Interest, Washington, DC, 2013.

Martin, Roger. *The Responsibility Virus,* Basic Books, New York, 2002.

Navarro, Peter. *The Money Game, Understanding the Principles of Economics,* Barnes & Noble Publishing, United States, 2005. Audio CD.

Ornstein, Allen C. and Hunkins, Francis P. *Curriculum - Foundations, Principles, and Issues,* Allyn and Bacon, Boston, 1988.

Pangle, Thomas L. *The Great Debate: Advocates and Opponents of the American Constitution,* The Teaching Company, CD, 2007.

Perot, H. Ross. *United We Stand: How We Can Take Back Our Country,* Hyperion Books, 1992.

Peterson, Peter G. *Running on Empty,* Farrar, Straus, and Giroux, NY, 2004.

Ridgley, Stanley K. *Strategic Thinking Skills*, audio CD.

Ricks, Thomas E. *Fiasco – The American Military Adventure in Iraq*, Penguin Books, New York, 2007.

Robert, Michael A. *Transformational Leadership: How Leaders Change Teams, Companies and Organizations*, The Teaching Company, audio CD, 2007.

Salemi, Michael K. *Money and Banking: What Everyone Should Know*, The Teaching Company, DVD. Lectures 1-16.

Schultz, Howard, with Joanne Gordon. *Onward*, Rodale, New York, 2011. (Note: This book reveals a possible framework or guide that can be used for instituting change within the government.)

Schiller, Bradley R. *The Macro Economy Today* – Tenth Edition, McGraw-Hill Irwin, New York, 2006.

Skousen, W. Cleon. *The 5,000-Year Leap, The 28 Great Ideas That Changed the World* , National Center for Constitutional Studies, United States, 2006.

Spaeth, Harold J. & Edward Conrad Smith. *The Constitution of the United States*, 13th edition, Harper Perennial, New York, 1991.

The Battle of Algiers.. Dir. Gillo Pontecorvo, (The Criterion Collection) 1966 DVD.

Titchener, Frances. *To Rule Mankind and Make the World Obey – A History of Ancient Rome,* Barnes & Noble Publishing, United States, 2004, audio CD.

William Bonner and Addison Wiggin. *The New Empire of Debt The Rise and Fall of an Epic Financial Bubble, 2nd Edition* , John Wiley & Sons, Inc., New Jersey, 2009.

Welch, Patrick J. and Welch, Gerry F. *Economics – Theory and Practice*, 7th edition, John Wiley & Sons, Inc., New Jersey, 2004.

Printed newspaper articles:

Associated Press, "Clinton cites Depression in balanced-budget attack." *Denver Post*, Feb 26, 1995.

Associated Press, "Clinton Defends Fund-Raising Tactics." *Post Standard*, Syracuse, Feb 27, 1997:A-3.

Associated Press, "Clinton Helps Raise Money." *Post Standard*, Syracuse, Feb 19, 1997:A-6.

Associated Press, "Perot blasts Clinton plan for Mexican bailout." *Rocky Mountain News*, Business, Jan 14, 1995:50A.

Associated Press, "U.S. Trade Gap Hits Near-Record Mark." *Post Standard*, Syracuse, Aug 18, 1995.

Associated Press, "High Court Rejects Arizona's 'Scarlet Letter' for Term Limits." *Post Standard*, Syracuse, Feb 25, 1997:A-5.

Bank, David, "Iomega to Slash 500-700 Utah Jobs In Shift to Malaysia." *Wall Street Journal*, Dec 31, 1996:p10.

Beck, Joan, "Welfare often hurts more than it helps." *Denver Post*, Jul 16, 1995.

Bounds, Gwendolyn, "The Case against a Higher Minimum Wage." *Wall Street Journal*, Small Business, Aug 3, 2004:B8.

Broder, David, "Budget-cut balloon is leaking." *Denver Post*, Jan 4, 1994:7B.

Buchanan, Patrick J., "Term limits — the key to revolution." *Denver Post*, Jul 8, 1997.

Gorman, Linda, " 'Trust fund' fraud dooms system." *Rocky Mountain News*, Commentary, Denver, May 14, 1995: 89A.

Greenberger, Robert S., "U.S. Current Account Deficit Swelled To Record $47.96 Billion in 3rd Period." *Wall Street Journal*, Dec 11, 1996: A2.

Greenwood, Daphne, "What if Congress had passed balanced-budget amendment?" *Denver Post*, May 27, 1995.

Hubbard, Burt, "Federal cuts could cost state millions." *Rocky Mountain News*, Denver, Jun 4, 1995: 4A, 16A.

Ivins, Molly, "Government Bought Buy Legal Bribes." *Post Standard*, Syracuse, Oct 19, 1996.

McQuaid, John, "Livingston leads budget-cutting charge." *Rocky Mountain News*, Denver, Dec 31, 1994.

Meltzer, Allan H., "Market Failure or Government Failure?" *Wall Street Journal*, Opinion, Mar 19, 2010: A19.

Montague, Bill, "Trade gap surge likely to continue." *USA TODAY*, Feb 20 1997: Sec B, p. 1.

New York Times News Service, "Boomers stuck in Social Security limbo." *Syracuse Herald American,* Dec 8, 1996: A11.

Paulsen, Michael S., "The Case for a Constitutional Convention." *Wall Street Journal,* May 3, 1995: A15.

Snow, Tony, "Is there truth in budgeting?" *Denver Post Standard*, Apr 9, 1995.

About the Author:

James S. Sitnik has a wide array of interests and work experiences. He has spent eight years in the military as a weather observer/forecaster in the Atmospheric Scientific Laboratories section of the US Army. He has spent significant time working in the retail and mutual fund industries; and he worked as a freelance videographer after graduating from the University of Utah with a degree in filmmaking. He has been working in the computer industry for the last 18 years.

Mr. Sitnik enjoys taking classes and reading about business management, leadership, economics, and music.

One of Jim's mantras is "Keep learning."

www.ingramcontent.com/pod-product-compliance
Lightning Source LLC
Chambersburg PA
CBHW071337280526
45787CB00001B/124